The Class 33s -

A Celebration of 30 Years

John Hypher

Dedicated to
Sian and Mark

Runpast Publishing, 10 Kingscote Grove, Cheltenham, GL51 6JX
Printed by: The Amadeus Press, Huddersfield.
Typeset by: P.P.S. - DTP Bureau, 11 Holtham Ave, Churchdown, GL3 2AR

ISBN 1 870754 19 0

Contents

Acknowledgements

I acknowledge with grateful thanks the following people and organisations who have contributed information, photographs, artwork or authority to reproduce copyright material for use in this book.

M Furnell; Martyn West; Simon Moore; M MacMillan; S Blackman; P Keer; Templecombe Station Promotion Group; Robin Brown of the Eastleigh and South Hants Weekly News; The Commanding Officer of HMS Sultan; G Bruder and C K Brooks of Sulzer Diesel; Keith Collins of British Rail, Western Region; Gary Smith of British Rail, Southern Region; Network SouthEast; Robin Pearson of The County of Avon; Rodney Lissenden; Peter Jaques; John Maddison; Len Shelton of The Borough of Eastleigh; Roger Harris for extracts from his *Allocation History of BR Diesels and Electrics*; R Hope of *The Railway Gazette*. Special thanks go to Paul Llewellyn, Mike Howell and Keith Dungate of the Class 33 Locomotive Club for their help and encouragement over several years and to John Scrace, the principal photographic contributor to this book for allowing me to freely draw from his extensive collection of Crompton photographs.

John Hypher

Front cover, top: D6534 is seen during the early 1960s in original green livery.

Photo: M. MacMillan

Front cover, middle left: 33107 approaches Waterloo in July 1984 at journey's end with the 0548 from Exeter St. Davids.

Photo: John Hypher

Front cover, bottom left: 83301 (alias 33115) is pictured at Basingstoke on 1 May 1990 whilst on a series of high speed test trains which ran between Basingstoke and Woking.

Photo: John Scrace

Front cover, bottom right: Railfreight Construction liveried 33204 was caught by the camera working wrong line on Hildenborough bank during April 1989.

Photo: Keith Dungate

Back cover: Prototype Crompton 33001 in its final death throes at Eastleigh TMD during February 1989.

Photo: Class 33 Locomotive Club Collection

D6508 and D6509 stand outside the Birmingham Railway Carriage and Wagon Company's works at Smethwick prior to delivery to the Southern in April 1960.
Photo: Class 33 Locomotive Club Collection

Chapter 1 In the Beginning

Over 30 years have now elapsed since what were to emerge as the 'Cromptons' were little more than a twinkle in the planners eyes. While steam reigned supreme, the embryo of the next generation of motive power was steadily growing. The basis of the new generation emerged in 1955 as the British Railways Modernisation Plan - one of the most significant landmarks in modern day railway history. The Plan, on the one hand signed the death warrant of the steam locomotive on Britain's railways, but on the other was to herald the birth of 98 type 3 diesel - electric locomotives - the 'Cromptons' - to which the history of this book is devoted.

The Birmingham Railway Carriage and Wagon Company of Smethwick was awarded contracts to build these locomotives for the Southern Region, with construction commencing during the early months of 1959. December saw the delivery of the prototype and within no time at all both railwaymen and enthusiasts alike had christened the new arrivals 'Cromptons' because of their Crompton Parkinson electrical equipment.

Orders for these type 3 Bo-Bo machines were placed with BRCW in four stages, the first for 45 locomotives being placed in December 1957. This was followed by an order for a further 20 in October 1958, 12 in July 1959 and the remaining 21 in October 1959. Specifications for the twelve machines ordered in July 1959 differed from their contemporaries in that they were to be specially constructed some eight inches narrower for use on the Hastings line with its restricted loading gauge. In the 'flesh' these were easily distinguished from their standard stablemates by their slab-sided appearance and narrower front cab windows. Almost predictably the nickname 'Slim Jims' was soon in common use. The necessity for the 'Slim Jims' can be traced back over a century to the 1850s when a story of fraud and greed unfolded on the part of the railway builders. Specifications for the tunnels through the Sussex Weald called for a lining of six layers of bricks, and it was not until 1862 when the Wadhurst Tunnel collapsed that the London and South Eastern Railway discovered that the contractors had in fact lined the tunnels with only four layers. The bore too was narrower than specified and the cost of rebuilding the tunnels to specification was found to be prohibitive. It was decided therefore to line them with two additional layers of bricks with the resultant loss of width. Those responsible for the fraud were subsequently charged, tried and imprisoned.

In basic design and outline, the Cromptons bear distinct similarities with their type 2 cousins (class 26) and in many ways are a derivative of this class which first entered service during the summer of 1958. They differed, however, in a number of respects from the type 3s (class 33), the most significant variations being their engine size, power, and method of train heating. Crompton Parkinson electrical equipment and Sulzer engines were fitted to both types but whereas the type 2s had 6 cylinder engines producing 1160 bhp, the type 3s incorporated the more powerful and larger 1550 bhp 8 cylinder engines.

Space under the type 2 'bonnet' was at a premium, yet the Cromptons were able to accommodate an additional two cylinders within the same size bodyshell. The answer lay in the method of train heating; the type 2s featuring a steam boiler whereas the type 3 incorporated an electric train heating (ETH) generator within the generator grouping. By eliminating the steam boiler, sufficient space was yielded to take on board the larger power unit. Specification of electric train heating by the Southern Region guaranteed their place in the history books by operating the very first main line ETH locomotives on British Railways.

Another wise choice was the larger power unit enabling the Cromptons to be truly versatile mixed traffic locomotives with duties ranging from branch line passenger trains to expresses and from slow unfitted goods formations to fitted block trains. The extra power obviated the need for wasteful double-heading except where particularly heavy loads or adverse gradients were involved.

The most significant body variations between the two types were the communicating doors fitted to each end of the class 26 locomotives and resultant small central windows on their cab fronts. The class 26 also had single line token catchers built in under the driver's side windows. The Cromptons by comparison featured a two-numeral headcode display placed centrally between the front cab windows and never carried communicating doors or token catchers.

As mentioned, Crompton deliveries commenced in December 1959 with the arrival of D6500 at Hither Green Depot which was indeed the first home for all 98 members of the class. New arrivals joined the strength at regular intervals of about one per week over the next two years or so concluding with the twelve narrow bodied 'Slim Jims', the last of which, D6597 entered service in May 1962. The whole class was delivered by a small group of Hither Green drivers who travelled 'pass' to Birmingham, lodged overnight and returned with their brand new charge the following day. Acceptance trials were carried out with each new locomotive before it entered service, this normally taking place on the main lines in Kent with a rake of coaches.

Standard machines were numbered consecutively from D6500 to D6585 and those built to the Hastings Line gauge followed on as D6586 to D6597. Over the years the Cromptons have been known by a number of classifications. Initially they were known as type 3s and designated KA by the Southern Region. However, following conversion to push-pull, the 19 locomotives so equipped were re-designated KB. When the new class system was introduced in 1968, the standard locomotives were classified 33/1, the push-pull machines 33/2 and the 'Slim Jims' as 33/3. This was soon changed though to 33/0, 33/1 and 33/2 respectively to coincide with their actual number series which were 33001 - 33065, 33101 - 33119 and 33201 - 33212. All but two of the original class of 98 locomotives were re-numbered, those missing having been withdrawn previously due to severe accident damage.

Duties of these versatile engines have been many and varied over the past 30 years or so, a wide spectrum of both freight and passenger work having been performed not only over Southern metals but over those of other regions too - notably the Western and London Midland. Passenger duties have comprised express, cross-country, main line, branch, inter-regional, excursion and boat trains, not to mention a wide assortment of specials. Freight trains too of almost every description have been worked by the class - from mixed unfitted freights and engineering trains to Freightliners and block trains carrying oil, cement and stone. More recently, they have been heavily utilised on the construction traffic for the Channel Tunnel ranging from single heading to triple headers. Whatever the task, the Cromptons have been

D5300

1B
D6544

very much at home and well able to handle the variety and demands placed upon them over the years.

Only a matter of months after the last Crompton was delivered, The Birmingham Railway and Carriage and Wagon Company sadly closed its doors for the last time owing to insufficient further orders being placed to ensure the Company's continued viability.

Now alas, after more than a quarter of a century's faithful service, the Cromptons in turn, now await their final journey to the cutter's torch. Some have already taken that fateful path, others are ready to go. A few will live on for construction and departmental duties and hopefully some will be preserved. Their demise in many ways will be mourned with no less a sense of loss than that which was felt a generation ago with the passing of steam. The Cromptons have served as a remarkable tribute to a great company that produced a truly fine locomotive. They have not only stood the test of time but also given consistent and invaluable service to their owners. The design, workmanship, quality and on-going standard of maintenance speaks for itself.

I hope this book will in some measure capture the true spirit of the 33 class and reflect the work they have so ably done, the wide ranging places they've been, their character and indeed the important part they have played in over 30 years of service with British Rail.

Top Left: BRC&W Type 2 (later Class 26) No. D5300 seen prior to delivery in 1958.

Photo: Courtesy Sulzer Diesel

Bottom Left: D6544 at Hither Green Depot when only a few weeks old in March 1961.

Photo: Courtesy Sulzer Diesel

D6507 photographed when new at Folkestone Junction with a Dover to Charing Cross train in June 1960.

Photo: Rodney Lissenden

Left: Wooden cab mock-up of a type 3 at the BRC&W Works.
Photo: Class 33 Locomotive Club Collection

Right: A couple of Cromptons under construction at the BRC&W Works.
Photo: Class 33 Locomotive Club Collection

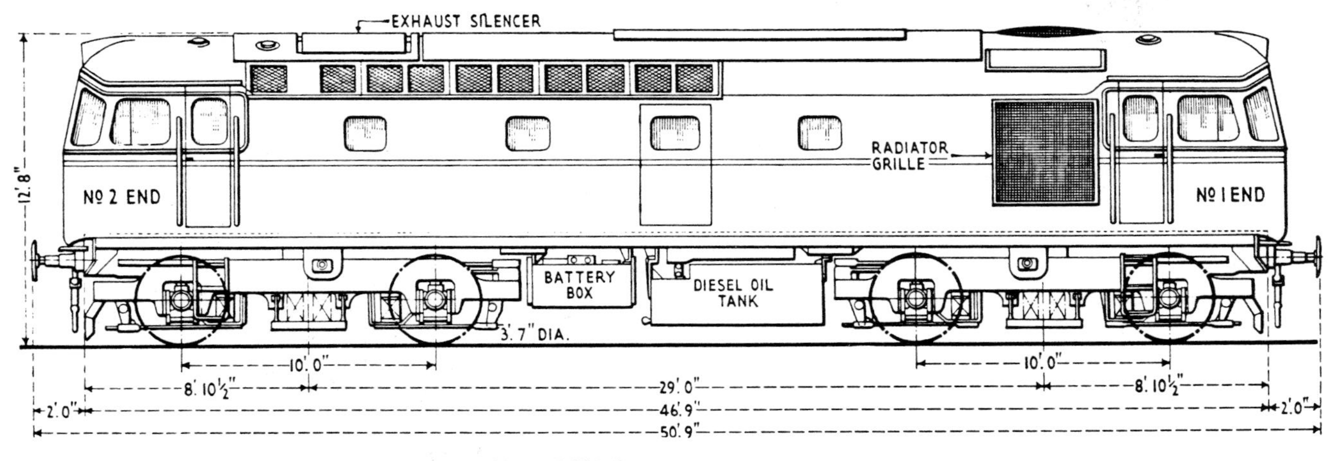

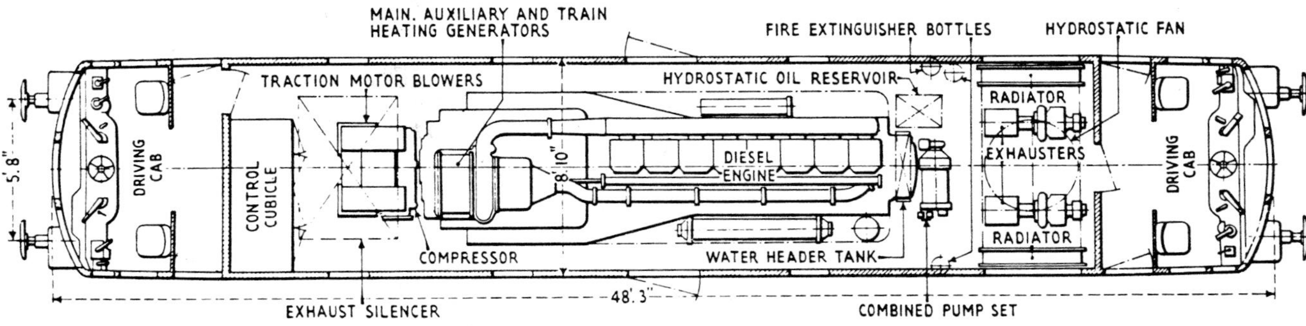

Diagram of the locomotive showing principal dimensions.

Courtesy: The Railway Gazette

Chapter 2 The Nuts and Bolts

Beneath their elegant exteriors, the Cromptons are complex machines comprising an amalgam of Birmingham Railway Carriage and Wagon Company design and construction, Sulzer mechanical engineering and Crompton Parkinson electrical engineering. This chapter systematically examines the locomotive in detail and provides a guided tour around the machinery and components that make it 'tick'.

The Body

The most familiar aspect of the locomotive is its bodyshell. Within this shell are housed the diesel engine, generator grouping and driving controls together with an array of equipment necessary to make the loco into a functional machine capable of carrying out the many demands placed upon it. The bodysides and underframe are of integral construction. Made up of welded steel, the underframe comprises two longitudinal double channel members joined by four transoms strategically located beneath the power unit and the bogie pivot centres. At each end of the frame is fitted a fabricated dragbox to which is fitted the drawgear and Oleo buffers. Welded to the mainframe are 'I' section steel girders fitted both vertically and diagonally forming the body frame to which are secured the steel plate body panels. Inspection access doors incorporating a small plain glass window are sited amidships along each side of the body together with three additional windows along each side to provide extra light for the engine room.

A series of ventilation grilles are situated at cantrail level with the large grilles on the bodysides (at no. 1 end) providing the inlets for the locomotive's cooling system. Indeed, it is these grilles which readily identify no. 1 end from no. 2 end.

The main bulkheads are situated behind the cab areas at each end of the locomotive and incorporate access doors into the engine room. Fibreglass roof panels are fitted, with those over the power unit/generator grouping being removable to allow unit removal when required. These particular panels are also translucent to provide additional light into the engine room. The cabs themselves are double skinned, the outer one being a one-piece construction. Two particular apertures in the roof are noteworthy. The first of these, placed towards the centre, is the exhaust vent. When new, these were originally located closer to no. 2 end. The other, a somewhat larger circular aperture at no. 1 end, houses the hydrostatically driven fan which forms an important part of the cooling system. The small oblong apertures at the front ends above each cab house the two-tone horns.

The Engine

The Cromptons are fitted with a Sulzer 8 cylinder 8LDA28-A turbo-charged diesel engine. These were manufactured under license by Vickers Armstrong of Barrow-in-Furness and have a continuous rating of 1550 bhp at 750 rpm. Their firing order is 1-4-7-3-8-5-2-6. Turbo-charging is effected by a Sulzer/De-Haviland LAG37-17 turbo-charger. Weighing-in at 12.25 tons, they are unique on British Rail in being the only 8 cylinder Sulzer engines to have been purchased. Their lubricating oil capacity is 108 gallons. Cooling is achieved by the Serck system which incorporates a hydrostatically driven, thermostatically controlled fan which is built into the roof and which automatically controls the speed of rotation of the cooling water. Air is drawn to the main radiators through the large body-side grilles at no. 1 end of the locomotive. Some 225 gallons of water circulates through the system to cool the engine and 12 gallons of oil are used to power the roof mounted fan. This fan cuts in at 167°F at which point the by-pass valve begins to close, allowing the oil to power the fan motor. As the temperature increases, the valve closes enabling more oil to pass through and when 175°F is achieved the valve is fully closed and the fan rotates at its maximum speed of 1310 rpm. To protect the engine from damage through adverse conditions occurring, an automatic shut-down system operates if the engine overspeeds, or if the oil or coolant pressures drop too low. Where overheating occurs, a light on the driver's panel comes on. A problem which has beset the Cromptons in recent years has been the cracking of no. 9 'A' frame on the crankcase. Whilst many have been repaired at either Derby or Crewe, the cost of repair and the down-time involved has brought about premature withdrawals and the exchanging of power units between locomotives where the general body condition of the recipient has been better than that of the donor.

The Generators

Attached to the drive shaft from the engine is the generator group which comprises three Crompton Parkinson generators each with its own distinct function.

The main generator, type CG391B1 is a self-ventilating, single bearing 10 pole machine with separately excited, self excited decompounding and starting windings giving a continuous rating of 1012kw and 1760 amps at 750 rpm. This produces up to 575 volts to power the four traction motors which are situated within the bogies.

The auxiliary generator, type CAG193A1, is a single bearing 8 pole machine continuously rated at 57kw and 518 amps at 450 rpm producing 110 volts to power a variety of equipment on the locomotive. These include the Davies and Metcalf air brake compressor (Crompton Parkinson C63B5), Reavell vacuum exhausters (Crompton Parkinson C72A1), Aerex traction motor blowers (Crompton Parkinson C64B3), Serck radiator fan motors, combined pump set (Crompton Parkinson C63A4), cab heaters, demisters and locomotive lights as well as charging the batteries.

Train heat is derived from the third generator in the grouping. Designed to produce 750 volts at any speed from 525 to 750 rpm, the ETH generator, type CAG392A1 is a 10 pole machine continuously rated at 250kw and 313 amps at 750 rpm. When train heating is required, the engine automatically maintains a minimum idling speed of 525 rpm (as opposed to its normal idling speed of 325 rpm) which is the lowest speed at which the heating can work.

When coupled in multiple, train heat is provided by the trailing - or train-locomotive. The ETH rating of a class 33 is 48 which at a value of 4 for each Mk1 coach will heat a 12 coach train. Electrical control equipment was supplied by Allen West and Company and is located behind the bulkhead at no. 2 end.

Other vital pieces of equipment in the engine room are the Aerex traction motor blowers powered by Crompton Parkinson electric motors. Air is forced via ducting formed inside the underframe longitudinals to the traction motors to keep them well ventilated and avoid overheating.

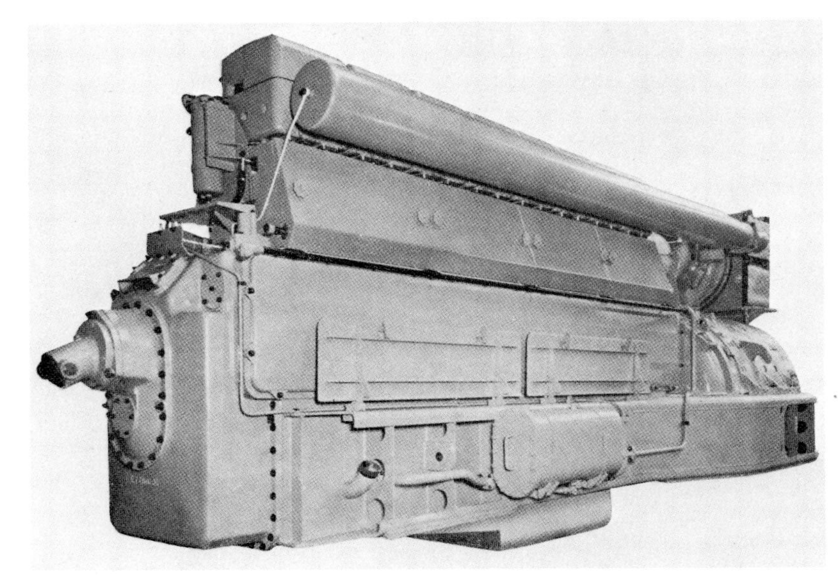

8LDA28-A Engine.

Photo: Courtesy Sulzer Diesel

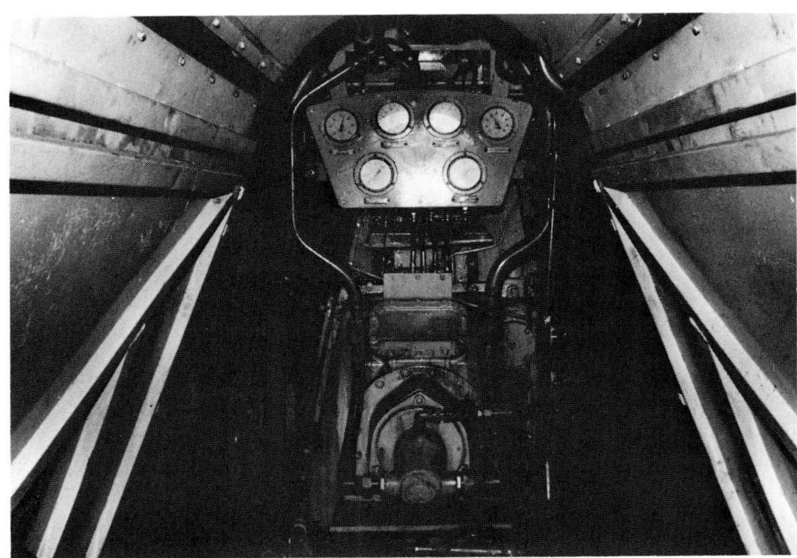

A somewhat dark view inside the engine room of a 33/1 as seen from No. 1 end.

Photo: John Hypher

View taken inside the engine room of the same locomotive as seen from the generator (No. 2) end.

Photo: John Hypher

The engine room is protected by a fire alarm circuit and sensors. In the event of fire breaking out, an alarm bell rings in each cab and the Sulzer engine automatically shuts down. Carbon dioxide gas CO_2 is simultaneously discharged from bottles located throughout the engine room. If fire breaks out in a class 33/1 locomotive whilst being driven from a remote driving trailer, the bell will continue to ring in the locomotive to let the driver know that the system has been activated. No separate warning is received in the trailer cab.

The Cabs

Before looking at the bogies and other equipment beneath the body, it is appropriate to take a look inside the driving cabs at the controls and layout.

Cromptons are driven from either cab and as such, the layout and controls at each end are identical. Within each cab the driving controls are duplicated on the right hand side enabling the locomotive to be driven from either position. The main driving position, however, is on the left where the control desk and instrument panel is situated. On each side of the cab, by the drivers feet, is the 'Dead mans' equipment or Drivers Safety Device. This comprises treadles which must remain depressed while the train is moving or indeed stationary with forward or reverse direction selected. If sufficient pressure is not maintained, the train brakes are applied and power to the traction motors is cut off. A seven second delay is built into the system to allow the driver to move from one side of the locomotive to the other.

The Automatic Warning System (AWS) is activated by means of sensors situated between the tracks. The receiving equipment on the locomotive tells the driver audibly what signal he is approaching. When a green signal is being approached a bell rings in the cab but if an amber or red light is showing a horn is sounded. The driver has three seconds to cancel the warning before the train brakes are applied.

The photographs on pages 12 and 13 show the controls and equipment in the cabs of each of the Crompton sub-types.

The Bogies and Traction Motors

Sitting under each end of the locomotive are the bogies, each comprising two axles. It is the bogie and axle arrangement which gives the locomotive its wheel arrangement designation - in this case Bo-Bo. This signifies two bogies each with two powered axles.

The bogies are held in position by means of centrally placed cast steel pivots and are capable of traversing a minimum curve of four chains. They are of the equalising beam type with spring bolsters and powered axles; their main frame being constructed from box-section welded steel. Four nests of helical springs support the equalising beam to the frame, while the main bogie bolster is supported on four suspension links which in turn are sprung by elliptical leaf springs.

Before wholesale withdrawals commenced, about one quarter of the class were fitted with mini-snowploughs attached to the bogies. In winter, two outer and one centre plough are carried, the centre one normally being removed during the summer months. The push-pull locomotives however have never carried mini-ploughs owing to the operational impracticalities they would present.

Traction is provided by four Crompton Parkinson C171C2 electric motors - one per axle which are axle-hung and nose suspended to the bogie frames. Their continuous rating is 305 hp at 580 volts and 440 amps. They are 4 pole machines, series wound and connected in parallel across the main generator. Cooling is achieved by force ventilation from blower motors situated in the engine room.

Class 33s are designed to operate either air or vacuum braked trains by means of an automatic brake valve; the system being known as dual braked. The locomotives themselves are air braked and when running light or with unfitted freight trains stop by means of their straight air brake. Air braked rolling stock works on the principle that compressed air at 70 psi in the braking system keeps the brakes off. Upon application of the train brake, air is released from the system causing the pressure to drop thus applying the brakes. Conversely on vacuum braked stock, it is the vacuum which keeps the brakes off. The exhauster creates 21 inches hg of vacuum in the train pipe and connections. This time, when the train brake is applied, air is progressively allowed into the system destroying the vacuum and creating the braking action.

Battery carriers - one each side, and the 750/800 gallon fuel tank are located between the bogies. In recent years, a number of Cromptons have been fitted with new 750 gallon tanks constructed at Eastleigh Works.

Conversions

Two notable modifications were carried out at Eastleigh Works in response to specific new traffic requirements; one being for passenger work and the other for freight. It was with the Bournemouth electrification scheme in mind that D6580 was modified for push-pull use during 1965 to test the feasibility of such use with this class. High level air pipes and 27 way jumper cables were fitted to the front ends which together with a 'Westcode' converter enabled the locomotive to be driven from a remote driving trailer. A period of extensive testing took place on the region both in passenger service and on controlled tests, the success of which culminated in the decision to convert a further 18 locomotives. The first 'production' example, D6521 (33108) was completed in November 1966 with others steadily joining the ranks during 1967 concluding with D6528 (33111) in November of that year. Prototype D6580 (33119), which incidentally was the only push-pull equipped locomotive to run in green livery, was modified to conform to its partners and was the last to be outshopped at the end of November 1967. 'Production' modifications including the fitting of buck-eye couplings, vestibule rubbing plates and retractable buffers as well as high level control jumpers and air pipes. They were also fitted with 'Loudaphone' intercoms enabling communication between the driver and guard. Starter bells were also added. As previously mentioned, the locomotive can be driven from a remote driving trailer by means of a 'Westcode' translator. Its function is to control the engine speed from commands given by the 4 position controller in the electric multiple unit (EMU) cab. These positions are shunt, series, parallel and weak field and the electric commands are translated via electro-pneumatic valves into differing air pressures which will run the engine at 430, 570, 720 and 750 rpm. The engine can also be started remotely from the EMU driving cab and a signal will tell the driver when this has been satisfactorily completed. The push-pull Cromptons, known among some enthusiasts as 'Bagpipes', are extremely versatile and can be positioned anywhere in the train formation and controlled from a remote cab.

The other modification carried out at Eastleigh was the fitting of slow-speed control equipment to the class 33/2

'Slim Jim' locomotives for use on the Mountfield - Northfleet gypsum trains. This apparatus enables the locomotive to be driven at a maximum speed of 3 mph when required. At Northfleet a continuous speed of mph is required for discharging the load. This speed is attained by means of a small box fitted to the trailing axle at no. 2 end containing a 100 tooth wheel which drives a Hawker Siddeley thyristor chopper control unit. An additional orange coloured speedometer box is fitted to the left of the driver in each cab showing mph calibrations to enable him to monitor the speed precisely. The first to be outshopped was 6592 (33207) in September 1969 followed by the rest of the sub class, with the programme concluding in March 1972 with the completion of 6588 (33203).

Cab layout of a standard 33/0.

Photo: Keith Dungate

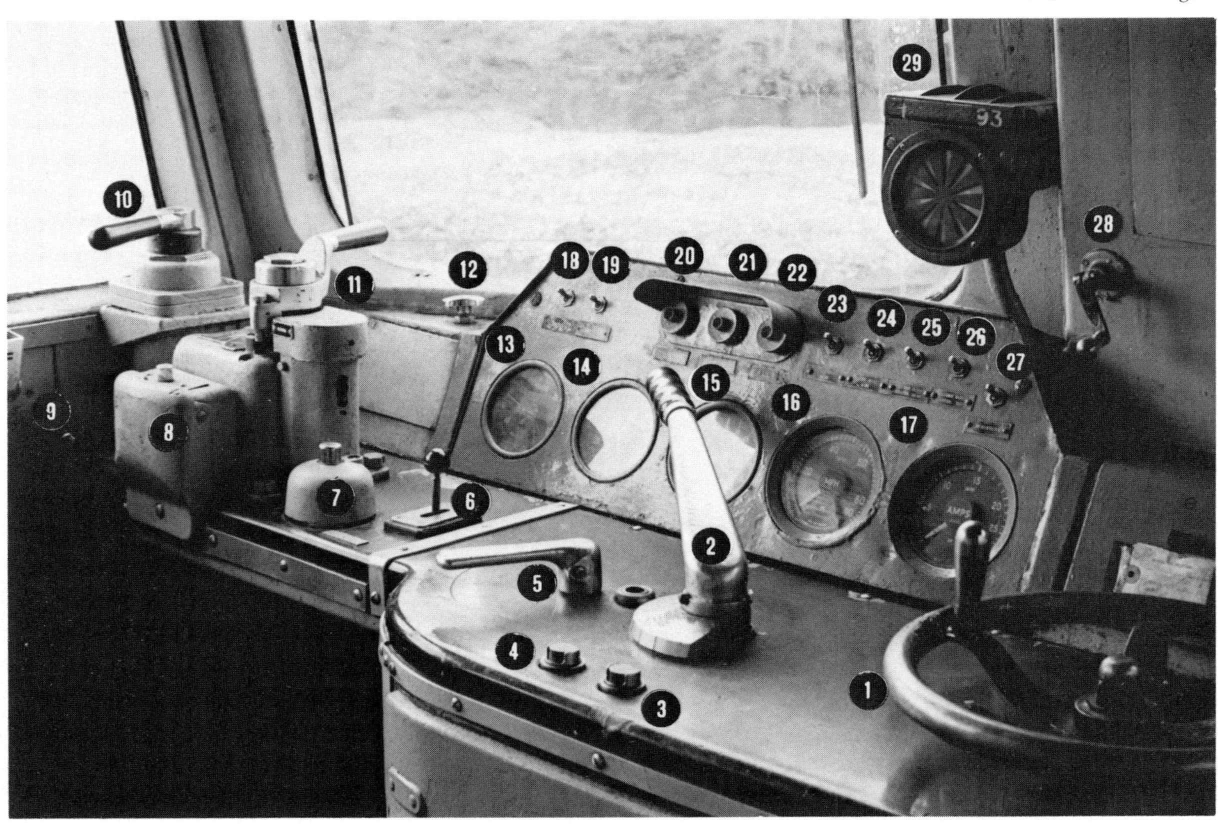

1 - Handbrake Wheel
2 - Power Handle
3 - Engine Stop Button
4 - Engine Start Button
5 - Master Switch
6 - Air Horn Valve
7 - AWS Reset Button
8 - Exhauster (Vacuum) High Speed Button
9 - Sanding Valve
10 - Loco Straight Air Brake
11 - Train Air/Vacuum Brake
12 - Windscreen Wiper Valve
13 - Main Reservoir/Brake Pipe Pressure Gauge
14 - Brake Cylinder Pressure Gauge
15 - Vacuum Gauge
16 - Speedometer
17 - Amp Indicator
18 - Route Indicator Light Switch
19 - Instrument Panel Light Switch
20 - Engine Light
21 - Wheel Slip Light
22 - Fault Light
23 - Driver's Heater
24 - Driver's Heater
25 - Second Man's Heater
26 - Second Man's Heater
27 - Demisters
28 - Route Number Handle
29 - AWS Sunflower Indicator
30 - Power Handle (Duplicate)
31 - Master Switch (Duplicate)
32 - Exhauster (Vacuum) High Speed Button
33 - AWS Reset Button
34 - Loco Straight Air Brake
35 - Train Air/Vacuum Brake
36 - Change End Switch
37 - Loudaphone Communication Set
38 - Slow Speed Demand Knob
39 - Slow Speed Speedometer (0 - 3 mph)

Cab layout - second man's side of a standard 33/0.

Photo: John Hypher

Cab layout of a push-pull 33/1.

Photo: Keith Dungate

Cab layout of a 'Slim Jim' 33/2.

Photo: Keith Dungate

Front layout of a standard class 33/0 locomotive.

Photo: Keith Dungate

1 - 27 way Jumper Receptacle
2 - Engine Control Air Pipe
3 - Train Heating Receptacle
4 - Main Reservoir Pipe
5 - Vacuum Pipe
6 - Brake Pipe
7 - AWS Receiver
8 - Electric Train Heat Jumper
9 - 27 way Control Jumper
10 - Main Reservoir High Level Pipe
11 - High Level Brake Pipe
12 - 27 way Jumper Receptacle
13 - Socket for Bell/Lamp unit
14 - Vestibule Rubbing Plate
15 - Oleo Retractable Buffers
16 - Buck-eye Coupling
17 - Sand Box
18 - Battery Carrier
19 - Fuel Tank
20 - Slow Speed Control Unit (33/2 class only)

Front layout of a push-pull class 33/1 locomotive.

Photo: John Hypher

Underframe view of a class 33/2 'Slim Jim'.

Photo: John Hypher

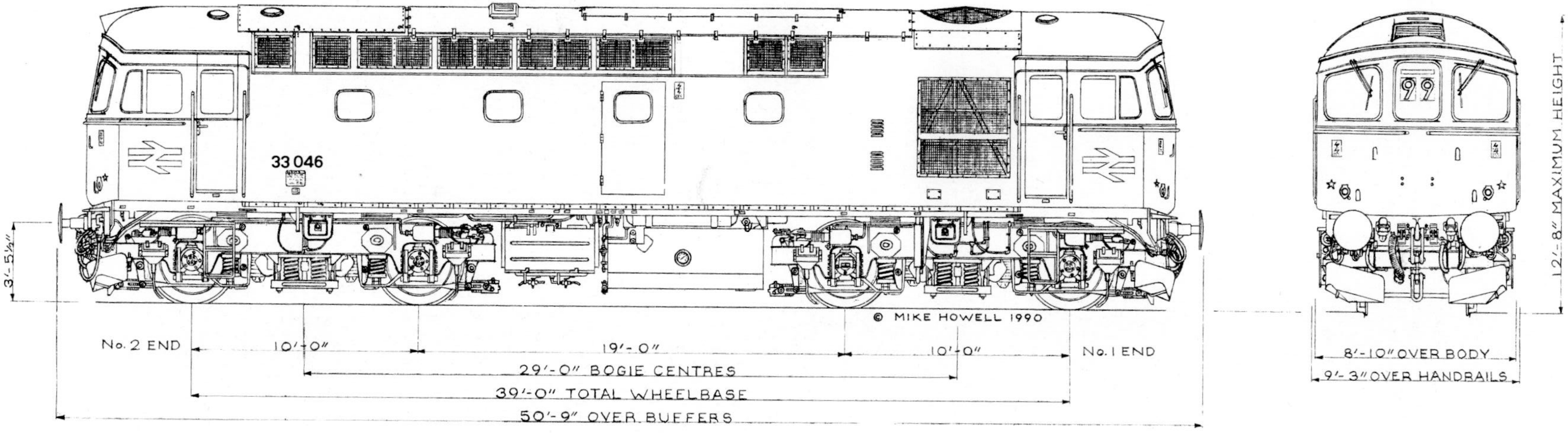

B.R.C.&W. TYPE 3 1550 BHP LOCOMOTIVE CLASS 33/0 No. 33046 AS RUNNING IN 1984

BRCW Type 3 1550 bhp Locomotive Class 33/0 No. 33046 as running in 1984.

Drawing: Mike Howell

Locomotive Details

Weight	33/0 76t 9cwt; 33/1 77t 6cwt; 33/2 76t 5cwt
Tractive effort	45,000 lbs max 26,000 lbs continuous
Wheelbase	39 ft
Bogie wheelbase	10 ft
Wheel diameter	3 ft 7 in
Bogie centres	29 ft
Width over body	8 ft 10 in (33/2 - 8 ft 2 in)
Width over handles	9 ft 3 in (33/2 - 8 ft 8 in)
Overall length	50 ft 9 in
Overall height	12 ft 8 in
Minimum curve negot.	4 chains
Maximum speed	85 mph (60 mph for most locomotives from Jan. 1990)
Sand capacity	2 cwt
Coupling code	Blue star (up to 3 locomotives can be driven in multiple from the leading locomotive)

D6502 and D5012 double-head a down Boat Train from Victoria to Dover via Chatham. This April 1960 view was taken near St. Mary Cray Junction.

Photo:Rodney Lissenden

Tonbridge is the setting for D6517 as it heads the 0910 Charing Cross to Ramsgate in August 1960.

Photo: John Scrace

Chapter 3 The First Decade - The 1960s

The new decade heralded the introduction of new motive power destined to serve the Southern for over thirty years in a variety of roles. The arrival of the Cromptons was very timely in that they were quickly put to work as an interim measure on passenger trains from London to the Kent Coast pending completion of the electrification scheme. As new locomotives arrived they were allocated to Hither Green Depot. Summer 1960 saw the type 3s earning their keep covering many of the weekday trains from Charing Cross to Folkestone, Dover and Ramsgate via Tonbridge and Ashford. Additionally, they powered boat trains from Victoria to Dover and Folkestone. Their stay, however, was relatively short-lived as the new electric service, albeit on the steam running times, was introduced some twelve months ahead of schedule in June 1961. Only signalling and further engineering work remained outstanding prior to the new timetables being introduced a year later. Indeed, The Cromptons proved useful on engineering trains along those sections of route being prepared for the new services.

They were also used on Maidstone East to Ashford and Ashford to Ramsgate services until Autumn 1961 together with trips between Appledore and New Romney.

At the other end of the scale they enjoyed brief spells of glory heading such famous trains as 'The Golden Arrow', 'Night Ferry' and 'Man of Kent'.

During those early years, winter time proved to be something of a headache as far as passenger workings were concerned as much of the available rolling stock was not equipped for electric train heating; this being the only form on offer from the Cromptons. The BR-Sulzer type 2 locomotives (later class 24) which had been on loan from the London Midland Region since 1959 came to the rescue and were double-headed with the type 3s over the first winter - not so much for their power - but for their steam which enabled the indigenous steam heated stock to be heated. This was effective in maintaining service but wasteful in terms of motive power as the type 2s were often simply mobile boilers other than on those occasions where their extra horse-power was required on heavy trains. The type 2s were duly returned to their rightful owners during 1962. As a last resort some trains had to be steam hauled until the warmer weather arrived.

As more of the class were delivered and others became available following release from passenger work, they progressively took over South Eastern freight duties. Within about a year they were covering a significant amount of freight movements in Kent including much of the cement traffic from Cliffe, Grain oil trains and Hoo branch work generally. Tied in with their freight duties were passenger trips between Gravesend and All Hallows. One of the more significant freights began operating in August 1961. This was the Cliffe (Kent) to Uddingston (Scotland) fully fitted cement train. Bearing the familiar 4A headcode, the type 3s soon ran as far as York via the East Coast main line, through workings commencing from December following a period of Eastern Region crew training. Initially, these runs were double-headed but experience proved that a single locomotive could adequately handle the load so after about a year the practice of double-heading ceased. For a while at least, the Eastern Region made good use of the Crompton during its layover, on a fill-in turn between York and Hull.

Various Cromptons were used between 1961 and 1963 for training Eastern Region drivers in connection with the through working to York and several short term transfers took place as follows to facilitate this.

Finsbury Park Depot:	11/61	D6559
New England Depot:	11/61	D6556
	12/61	D6517, D6559
	10/62	D6541
	7/63	D6553

Summer 1961 heralded the long if not fitful association of the class with the 'Kenny Belle's' which ran from Clapham Junction to Kensington Olympia on Mondays to Fridays during the peaks. The modern day push-pull operation with 4TC stock is a far cry from the old ex-SECR coaches which were still in harness when the Cromptons started running on this short but interesting 3 mile inter-regional service. Indeed, the honour fell to the 'Kenny Belle's' to be the very last diagramed passenger service for the class in 1989.

With the Kent Coast Electrification scheme all but complete, and a re-appraisal of freight requirements having been carried out, a number of type 3s were surplus to the needs of the Southern Eastern Division. As a result, 1962 saw the Cromptons spreading their wings and breaking the Hither Green monopoly with a migration westwards to Eastleigh on the South Western Division. Crew training began in the spring and within a few months some dozen or so of these locomotives were installed in their new home. Brought in to help the phasing out of steam traction on freight traffic, their duties developed to include a wide variety of local, departmental, regional and inter-regional freights, a prime source of work being oil trains from the large refinery at Fawley near Southampton. These started almost immediately and soon were heading to a number of diverse destinations. In less than a year their sphere of operation was quite extensive and continued apace. Regular trips to develop were those from Fawley to Bromford Bridge in the West Midlands. By November 1963 northbound trains were double headed to cope with the 2000 ton load which reputedly stretched for some quarter of a mile! Southbound empties however were split into two single-headed trains because of couplings having broken due to brake shocks en-route. To enable the Cromptons to work through to Bromford Bridge, D6518/20 and D6538 were despatched to Worcester Shrub Hill in January 1963 for a short spell of crew training, with through workings starting in March. Training took place on both freight and passenger trains and while on the latter the type 3s worked in tandem with a steam locomotive for train heating.

Bournemouth and Cromptons have been synonymous for many years. Their migration westwards in 1962 saw them make a somewhat modest debut on the Waterloo-Bournemouth-Weymouth line. But from small beginnings, their use increased progressively with the run-down of steam prior to the electrification of the line to Bournemouth in July 1967. They were regular visitors to the now demolished Bournemouth West Station which was sited close to the present Bournemouth EMU Depot, where the Cromptons for the Weymouth line were stabled for over two decades.

Southampton, long famed for its boat trains to the docks where the giants of the shipping world once berthed, saw the Cromptons using the tramway to enter the docks where they

D6542 at Shortlands with the 1400 Victoria to Folkestone Harbour in May 1961.

Photo: John Scrace

D6524 and D5007 double-head a down 'Golden Arrow' between Beckenham Junction and Shortlands during May 1961.

Photo: Rodney Lissenden

Sharnal Street is the setting for this November 1961 view of D6528 as it heads a Gravesend Central to Allhallows branch train.

Photo: Rodney Lissenden

were dwarfed by the visiting liners. Summer Saturdays also saw them connecting with ships of a smaller stature in the shape of the Lymington - Isle of Wight ferries on the Waterloo - Lymington Pier service.

Always game for heading named expresses, the type 3s made sporadic appearances on the famous ' Bournemouth Belle' and after an absence of many years have latterly headed the resplendent VSOE 'Bournemouth Belle' Pullmans on summer Saturdays during 1986 and 1987.

As with their first winter in Kent, the rolling stock situation generally continued to be a limiting factor for the class as regards passenger use. For the next few winters, the type 3s saw relatively little passenger activity owing to their inability to heat the available stock. Dual heated coaches were drafted in as other regions could spare them and this eased the problem to a certain extent.

In the meantime, the remaining Southern division, the Central, was not being neglected and by 1963 had built up a respectable amount of Crompton hauled freight traffic particularly in the London area and on the cross-country Ashford - Tonbridge - Redhill - Reading line. Indeed, by 1964 over thirty of the class were engaged on Central Division duties. The twelve 'Slim Jims' were delivered in 1962, their special loading gauge being for the Tonbridge - Hastings line where their primary use was on vans, mail and freight traffic.

D6559 is seen at Upper Warlingham with a Race Special from Victoria to Lingfield during May 1963.

Photo: John Scrace

May 1963 brought the type 3s to pastures new on Oxted line passenger services. They ran on a number of trains from Victoria or London Bridge to Tunbridge Wells West, East Grinstead and Brighton via Uckfield. Additional local services in the area sometimes took these locomotives from Tunbridge Wells West to Three Bridges or to Eastbourne via Eridge and from Three Bridges to East Grinstead. Various trips were also worked between Eastbourne and Hailsham. It was indeed on Oxted line services for spells during the latter part of 1965 and the early part of 1966 that the prototype push-pull locomotive, D6580 was put through its paces with 6TC trailer set no. 601 which was made up of surplus vintage EMU stock. This locomotive was converted in June 1965 and was the only push-pull machine to run in green livery. Prior to prototype service testing on the Oxted line, push-pull testing with a specially wired Crompton had been carried out the previous year between Wimbledon and Farnborough and between Victoria and Dover. These test runs together with a successful service performance heralded D6580 as the forerunner of the highly successful 33/1 sub class of 19 locomotives. Initial and exhaustive push-pull testing had been carried out with electro-diesel (later class 73) locomotives following which Ministry of Transport approval was given for propelling up to twelve coaches to a maximum speed of 90 mph. While never prolific on Oxted line passenger services, a remnant of class 33 operation remained during the morning and evening peaks between London Bridge, East Grinstead and Uckfield until May 1986.

Hither Green meanwhile was not only losing an increasing number of its charges to Eastleigh but to St. Leonards also where the 12 strong sub-class of 'Slim Jims' were based from July 1963 to October 1967.

The early years produced a number of interesting Crompton hauled passenger trains particularly on summer Saturdays. Among these were Brighton to Bournemouth, Brighton to Plymouth (as far as Salisbury), Margate to Wolverhampton (as far as Reading), Waterloo to Exeter and Waterloo to Swanage.

Summer 1963 marked the introduction of the class to several passenger workings on the Reading-Redhill-Tonbridge service where they variously plied alongside steam hauled services and diesel-electric 'Tadpole' multiple units until 1977.

Progress on the Bournemouth electrification during 1966/7 was continuing apace and during weekend engineers track occupations the Cromptons worked either singly or by piloting steam locomotives over the diversionary Mid-Hants (Watercress Line) route. Double-headed type 3s were not uncommon on Sunday 'Bournemouth Belle' expresses.

During 1966/7 Eastleigh Works was busy carrying out the push-pull modifications in readiness for their new role between Bournemouth and Weymouth. Some of these trains however were push-pull operated from December 1966, several months before the full switch to this mode of operation. As new 4TC units arrived for the Bournemouth line from the summer of 1966, they were put to work with the Cromptons

D6577 heads south near Potters Bar with the Uddingstone to Cliffe cement train in June 1963.

Photo: Rodney Lissenden

D6532 heads south in June 1963 with an empty oil train bound for Fawley near Oxford.

Photo: Rodney Lissenden

D6502 lies on its side at Itchingfield Junction following a collision with another freight train. Taken over two weeks later on 22nd March, 1964, this loco was eventually cut up on site.

Photo: John Scrace

D6548 on the 1604 Redhill to Reading at Dorking Town during September 1964.

Photo: John Scrace

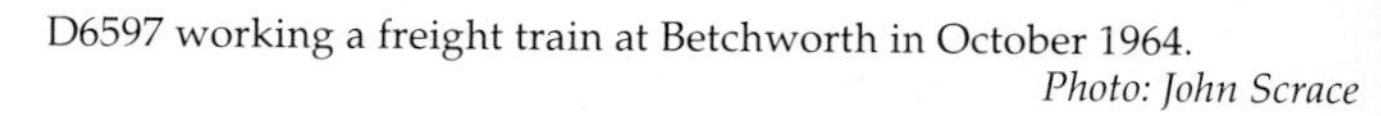

D6597 working a freight train at Betchworth in October 1964.

Photo: John Scrace

and used in conventional loco hauled formation. Some of the TCs however comprised only three coaches for a while so that the complete trains could be accommodated within the platform lengths. For several months prior to full electrification and also for a while afterwards pending deliveries of the remaining 4REP tractor units and to overcome initial teething problems, class 73 electro-diesels also worked alongside the type 3s on Bournemouth line services. D6580 together with new TC units were high speed tested on the Bournemouth line during August 1966 following which crew training commenced. December ushered in the first 'production' push-pull services between Waterloo and Bournemouth, initially using D6521 which was the first to be released and the first to receive the new blue livery. Trains operating on this basis were a temporary measure and remained relatively few in number. As new TCs were outshopped, Cromptons made a number of sorties to York to fetch their eagerly awaited retinues. They also journeyed north in the company of a TC unit to collect new 4REP tractor units, working in push-pull mode.

Towards the end of 1966 the Crompton-TC partnership ventured onto the West of England main line with trips being made between Salisbury, Basingstoke and Waterloo. Indeed on summer Saturdays during 1965 Cromptons were kept busy on Waterloo-Exeter services and during the latter part of the 1960s it was not uncommon to see the 33s covering for failed 'Warships' on this line, their taking over completely from 1971.

Electrification of the Waterloo-Bournemouth line officially took place in July 1967, with services between Bournemouth and Weymouth firmly in the capable hands of the push-pull 33/1s and their constant companions the class 491 4TCs until May 1988. In the absence of electrification where full economies could be made, this combination posessed many of the advantages of a multiple unit and made efficient use of rolling stock and motive power enabling the through service between Waterloo and Weymouth to run with minimal delays and inconvenience to users. The usual formation of the 12 car electric multiple units from Waterloo to Bournemouth comprised 4TC + 4TC + 4REP, the latter always being positioned at the London end other than during severe weather conditions. On arrival from London, the leading 4 or 8TC units were detached at Bournemouth and continued their journey to Weymouth behind a push-pull Crompton, this being situated at the Weymouth end. On the return leg, the train was driven from the cab of the leading TC unit and then attached to the unit(s) waiting in the 'up' platform at Bournemouth for London. The Swanage branch which diverged from the Weymouth line at Worgret Junction, and which closed in January 1972, was also served by 33/1s and 4TCs. Normal traction however on this branch was provided by class 205 DEMUs following the end of steam.

D6575 on a freight from Woking Yard at Deep Cut near Purbright in March 1966.

Photo: Rodney Lissenden

Diverted due to engineering work, D6540 is seen at Butts Junction, Alton with the 1330 Waterloo to Weymouth during May 1966.

Photo: John Scrace

D6528 passes New Milton with a down freight in June 1966.
Photo: John Scrace

D6541 heads the 0930 Waterloo to Bournemouth Central during March 1967. This train is seen at Brockenhurst.
Photo: John Scrace

A rare shot of the diverted 'Bournemouth Belle' at Aldershot captured during early 1967 with the Pullman train being double-headed.
Photo: M Furnell

Major classified overhauls have always been carried out at Eastleigh Works where an unrivalled expertise was developed on these locomotives. However, while Eastleigh was undergoing re-organisation and modernisation during the late 1960s a number of overhauls were carried out at Crewe.

The once familiar double-headed Crompton passenger services which ran on summer Saturdays between Brighton and Exeter with stock then proceeding to a variety of West of England destinations (this seemed to change annually) can trace their origins back to at least 1968 as can the almost prophetic trips between Portsmouth Harbour and Cardiff. The latter in 1968 comprised two round trips to the Principality but in 1969 ran double-headed on a morning train from Portsmouth Harbour, returning as two separate trains from Cardiff during the afternoon.

The 1960s saw the Cromptons running throughout on a number of specials and reliefs away from the Southern to such places as Parkestone Quay, Lowestoft, Birmingham, Norwich and Bristol, although inter-regional freight traffic had become quite common-place. Cross-London inter-regional freight movements were soon the order of the day, with the type 3s regularly visiting the London area yards of other regions. Right from the early days during the winter months it has been customary and indeed necessary for the Cromptons to assist electric multiple units during periods of severe weather where snow and ice had wreaked havoc with lines, rolling stock and current collection gear.

A number of the type 3s were temporarily transferred away from the Southern for various testing purposes during the early years. D6504 was loaned to Derby in February 1961 in connection with ETH equipment testing; this being the only class of diesel locomotive fitted with this type of heating at that time. Several test trips were carried out along the East Coast main line between London and Edinburgh with electrically heated Mk1 coaches. Three years later in January 1964, D6553 was also sent to Derby to take part in Freightliner braking tests. A Crompton was used because other available diesels were unable to provide braking for air braked rolling stock. Several round trips were made to Leicester with the loco returning south again at the end of the month. But no sooner had it returned to Hither Green, it was despatched to Swindon for a short spell during March.

Some early casualties among the fleet occurred during the 1960s, the first being D6502 which saw only about four years of service before being written off in an accident at Itchingfield Junction (Horsham) in March 1964. It had been working a Brighton to Three Bridges freight when it was in collision with another freight train. Damage was so extensive that it was cut up on site. 6576 was also written off after sustaining substantial accident damage at Reading Depot in 1968.

On a happier note though, modifications to the twelve 'Slim Jims' started at the end of the decade in October 1969 with the fitting of slow speed control apparatus in readiness for the Northfleet - Mountfield gypsum trains.

Medstead and Four Marks is the location of the diverted 1030 Waterloo to Bournemouth headed by D6550 during May 1967.
Photo: M Furnell

Chapter 4 The 1970s

Following their conversion to slow-speed control, the 'Slim Jims' began working the Mountfield to Northfleet merry-go-round gypsum trains as regular motive power from July 1970 for some 16 years before being relieved of their command by class 47s in October 1986. On arrival at Northfleet, these trains joined the merry-go-round circuit to discharge their loads while maintaining a constant speed of mph. The cement manufacturing plant at Northfleet is the largest in Europe and utilises large quantities of gypsum from the mines at Mountfield in the manufacturing process. With the electrification of the Hastings line which brought with it the singling of the offending stretches, the need for the narrow Cromptons was obviated.

Another major passenger route was opened to the class in October 1971 when they took over the Waterloo - Exeter services as principal motive power from the Western Region's diesel-hydraulic 'Warships'. Indeed, they managed to get in some practice beforehand on this route which stretches for almost 173 miles by covering for the ailing 'Warships' as these fell by the wayside and also by having worked summer Saturday duties. Despite the demands placed upon them, the Cromptons put in commendable service for almost nine years until May 1980 when the pendulum swung the other way and they in turn were replaced by the new generation of 'Warships' in the shape of the more powerful Western Region class 50s. But they didn't disappear entirely from the line, being utilised on short workings between Waterloo, Salisbury and Yeovil on both a push-pull and conventional basis.

The Western Region's covetous eyes on the Cromptons are not as recent as many might think and their use on both passenger and freight fill-in turns provided good utilisation for the class. An early example of the latter were trips on the Radstock branch from Frome in Somerset. From January 1972 they were booked to run on an afternoon passenger train between Exeter and Barnstaple as well as covering various journeys between Exeter and Newton Abbot via the famous sea wall at Dawlish. Beyond this, fill-in trips later brought the 33s to the seaside resort of Paignton.

Well-known for their summertime double headings, the class ran on the Brighton - West of England service until the end of the 1971 season before re-emerging again in 1977. As already mentioned, final destinations tended to change but the locomotives normally only worked through as far as Exeter.

The nominal summer Saturday class 33 trips between Portsmouth Harbour and Cardiff continued for several years and during 1972 and 1973 at least, token Sunday journeys were also made. The former year produced an interesting double header on the 11.20 trip from Portsmouth Harbour to Cardiff, with the locomotives running as far as Bristol Temple

Fawley is the setting for 6539 as it sets off with the 1545 oil train for Wolverhampton in July 1970.

Photo: John Scrace

6553 passes along the tramway at Canute Road, Southampton during July 1970.

Photo: John Scrace

Meads. One of these returned south in service at 17.50 while the other worked a vans train to Salisbury at 16.20. A noteworthy summer Saturday train during 1972 produced a double headed morning service from Weymouth to Temple Meads with a class 33 being piloted by a class 35 'Hymek'. The Crompton then returned at lunchtime with a service to Portsmouth Harbour which had originated at Cardiff. What must qualify as the second longest push-pull service trains for the class at just over 141 miles from Portsmouth to Cardiff occurred over several weekends during October and November 1971. Consisting of 33/1s and pairs of 4TC units, a number of trains ran through to Cardiff while others went as far as Bristol Temple Meads. This was to test this mode of operation on the service, the results of which while being satisfactory did not lead to the idea being pursued.

Summer 1976 saw another brief encounter with push-pull Cromptons and TC units on the Portsmouth - Bristol service together with trips between Eastleigh and Fareham, and Reading to Salisbury to cover shortages of 'Hampshire' diesel-electric multiple units.

Extension of push-pull running, this time on a more regular footing was introduced in October 1976 on two lines. These ran on Sundays from Portsmouth Harbour to Reading and from Waterloo to Salisbury. The Reading service, just over 63 miles in length, utilised a 33/1 together with a 4TC unit with the locomotive being placed at the Portsmouth end of the train. This continued for almost twelve years on a Sundays only basis until May 1988 when much of the Crompton passenger activity ceased. Surviving by a year until May 1989 were the Waterloo-Sailsbury/Yeovil 'shorts' which were push-pull initially on Sundays only. In May 1978 however, this was extended to include weekdays as well. Running in either 4 or 8TC formation, the locomotive was normally placed at the Salisbury end of the train.

Holidaymakers, locals and enthusiasts alike gathered along the Quayside to witness an unusual railway phenomenon along Weymouth Quay. For British Rail took to the roads with its Channel Islands Boat Trains to and from Waterloo. Trains have run along the Quay tramway since pre-grouping days and the turn of the Cromptons came in 1973 when following successful tests earlier in the year, they became a regular feature of the local scene for well over a decade. Some of the trains were hauled throughout by the 33s from Waterloo to the Quay Station while others were drawn between London and Bournemouth by electro-diesel class 73s or 74s 'on juice' drawing current from the third rail and handing over to a 33/1 for the final leg to the Quay. On arrival at Weymouth, the train ran adjacent to the Town Station before leaving BR property and taking to the streets. Before being let loose to compete with the town's motoring fraternity for road space,

6513 is seen at Parkstone Station with the 1015 inter-regional service from York to Poole in July 1971.

Photo: John Scrace

6567 is seen departing trom Reigate with the 1640 Redhill to Reading in July 1972.

Photo: John Scrace

6595 is seen during March 1973 with wagons of sand at Redhill.

Photo: John Scrace

6517 was caught by the camera at Brockenhurst during the summer of 1973 as it headed towards Bournemouth.

Photo: Mike Howell

6597 heads an inter-regional oil train at West Brompton on the West London Line during August 1973.

Photo: John Scrace

33051 surrounded by semaphore signals at North Kent West Junction during August 1974 while working the 1213 Norwood Yard to Hoo Junction.

Photo: John Scrace

33024 at Horsham with the 1204 Chichester to Norwood freight in May 1975.

Photo: John Scrace

the locomotive was fitted with a warning bell and orange flashing light which sat on the vestibule rubbing plate and plugged into a special socket on the front of the locomotive. All push-pull Cromptons were fitted with these sockets but latterly the flashing light units became self contained and were fitted to one of the lower lamp brackets. The train was joined by a British Transport Police escort and by two railwaymen carrying red and green flags respectively. The latter walked in front of the train to the Quay Station. For the return journey, the locomotive ran round its coaches and the warning equipment transferred to the other end. Escort arrangements were also repeated. These trains carried the headcode 90 in comparison with the regular push-pull service trains which generally carried 91 or 92. With the cessation of Channel Islands ferries from Weymouth, the boat trains stopped running in 1987.

Freightwise, the 33s were regularly working cement trains from Northfleet to Dunstable as far as Luton and hauling fuel tankers from the Fawley Refinery to Plymouth Laira Depot. The mid 1970s onwards also saw the class on Freightliner duties between Willesden and Southampton Freightliner terminals with all three operations producing double headers where the loads warranted this.

In 1974 an operating practice was in existence where two trains were joined at Basingstoke for their onward journey to Waterloo. An example during this year comprised the 0653 from Salisbury made up of a 33/1 locomotive and 4TC unit and the 0728 4VEP electric multiple unit (EMU) from Southampton which were coupled together to form the 0800 to Waterloo. This practice of joining a Crompton powered train with an EMU continued on a limited number of peak hour trains, particularly from Waterloo, until the late 1980s.

33041 met an untimely end as the result of a collision at Bricklayers Arms Junction with a 4SUB unit on 11 September 1975. The locomotive had been hauling a train of empty coaching stock from London Bridge to New Cross Gate just after the morning rush hour when the collision occurred with no. 4704 working in from Epsom Down to London Bridge. Damage was such that the locomotive was withdrawn and finally cut up at Selhurst early the following year.

A sunny May morning in 1977 saw 33021 at Wimbledon with the 1112 from Acton to Tolworth.

Photo: John Scrace

33117 complete with 4TC unit leaves Fareham with the 1728 from Fareham to Eastleigh in September 1978.

Photo: John Scrace

Framed at Clapham Junction, 33014 is heading the 1700 Waterloo to Exeter St. Davids during August 1978.

Photo: John Scrace

33002 and 33044 double-head the 1300 Waterloo to Exeter St. Davids at Clapham Junction in September 1979.

Photo: John Scrace

HALL & CO LTD
77

Mottingham was the scene of another serious collision in which 33036 was written off. The accident happened on 11 October 1977 while 33036 and 33043 were double heading a cement train from Northfleet to Dunstable. A fully fitted train of hopper wagons being hauled by a pair of class 47s and travelling in the opposite direction had failed, but unbeknown to the crew, a wagon had derailed on catch points and was fouling the opposite line. The two Cromptons collided at speed with the wagon, sending 33036 into a nearby garden and severely damaging 33043. While the latter was rebuilt, 33036 was withdrawn as being beyond repair and was eventually cut up at Slade Green a couple of years later during the autumn of 1979.

By the mid 1970s, class 33s were working inter-regional trains from Poole to the North of England, normally running as far as Reading and returning with southbound trains. On occasions, the locomotive ventured to Birmingham New Street as indeed they often did when on relief duties. Although diagrammed Crompton haulage on these services ceased in 1982, they have deputised for class 47s and operated on relief trains to the present day.

During the 1970s a wide variety of inter-regional excursions and specials were worked throughout by the class. The following selection highlights the diverse destinations visited: Bournemouth to Worcester, Eastbourne to Norwich, East Croydon to Totnes, Brighton to Kings Lynn, Watford Junction to Paignton, Bournemouth to Barry, Gravesend to Torquay, Portsmouth to Birmingham, Folkestone to Cambridge, Brighton to Peterborough, Brighton to Spalding, Clapham Junction to Swansea, East Croydon to Barnstaple, East Croydon to Abergavenny and Ramsgate to Bath.

On 5 September 1979, Lord Mountbatten's funeral train was entrusted to two members of the class, 33027 and 33056 for its journey to Romsey in Hampshire. Both were immaculately turned out complete with the white Royal lamp on the front of the leading locomotive. A year later, both were again together at Waterloo gleaming as before but this time in a revised livery to be honoured at their naming ceremony where they were given the names 'Earl Mountbatten of Burma' and 'The Burma Star'.

Top Left: 33003 and 33023 arrive at Millbrook with the 1023 Freightliner from Willesden in September 1979.

Photo: John Scrace

Bottom Left: 33038 is pictured at East Croydon during September 1979 with the 1750 from London Bridge to East Grinstead.

Photo: John Scrace

Above: 33027 and 33056 are seen at Vauxhall with Lord Mountbatten's Funeral Train on 5th September 1979.

Photo: John Scrace

Chapter 5 The 1980s

The 1980s witnessed the Cromptons both reach their peak in terms of diagrammed passenger services and also their decline and demise. Indeed, by the autumn of 1989 they had totally disappeared from the passenger scene other than running a few specials or reliefs or covering for failures or non availability of various rostered motive power.

Following their departure from the Exeter line, the 33s were swiftly drafted onto the Portsmouth Harbour - Bristol - Cardiff service from May 1980 replacing in their wake many of the incumbent class 31s. A remnant of these however remained on the line until 1982 particularly between Bristol and Cardiff. Bearing the familiar '89' headcode, Cromptons pounded the Severn - Solent metals for eight years until falling victim to the class 155 'Sprinters' in May 1988. Stretching across some five English and Welsh counties from Hampshire to South Glamorgan, the Portsmouth service developed into a basic hourly headway on Mondays to Saturdays between Portsmouth Harbour and Bristol Temple Meads with a number of through trains working to Cardiff. The Bristol - Cardiff service was in the hands of varying motive power including Cromptons, DMUs and High Speed Trains which shared a regular frequency to and from the Principality. Sundays on the Portsmouth line were very much quieter by comparison and included some short workings between Portsmouth and Westbury which carried headcode '88' in the locomotive's indicator display.

At Bristol, through trains to or from Cardiff changed direction and required a change of locomotive. On arrival the Crompton was removed from one end and replaced by another at the other end to continue the journey. Portsmouth Harbour, on the other hand, being a dead end meant that on arrival the locomotive was trapped in the platform until the next locomotive arrived to take the train out again. The 33s took their layover at Fratton between trips and ran light engine to and from Portsmouth Harbour Station. The 'Portsmouths' opened up the way for a wide spectrum of other services, particularly in Wales.

During their reign on the busy and demanding Portsmouth line, the class still managed to sneak in a smattering of journeys on the Portsmouth to Salisbury stopping service which was a firm class 205 'Hampshire' unit stronghold; these being readily identified by the Headcode '87'.

Further horizons soon came into view with fill-in trips between Bristol and Weston-super-Mare together with weekday peak hour through services on the Weymouth line supplemented by Saturday workings and sporadic Sunday activity. Through trains between Bristol and Weymouth tended to be few in number and between Cardiff and Weymouth even fewer, the service generally being entrusted to DMU's plying between Westbury and Weymouth and connecting into the Portsmouth service. Crompton fortunes were somewhat mixed on this line with their requirements tending to vary year by year. Consistent almost to the end however were early morning and late afternoon or early evening through trains on weekdays to and from Weymouth or Yeovil which displayed headcode '64'. While the majority of duties were inter-worked with the Portsmouth diagrams, latterly their weekend push-pull duties in particular originated from the Bournemouth area. While weekday trips along the 87 mile route were confined mainly to the peaks, journeys diagrammed for Saturdays varied in number and times from one year to another. Sunday workings were spasmodic and never comprised more than a couple of round trips with several years producing no Cromptons at all. The 1988 summer season was the last to see Cromptons running a Sunday service to Weymouth, this being push-pull with TC units originating from Bournemouth.

Honor Oak Park is the setting for 33038 as it makes its way to Uckfield with the 1720 from London Bridge in May 1980.
Photo: John Scrace

33009 passes under the now demolished gantry at St. Denys with the 1615 Portsmouth Harbour to Cardiff in April 1981.
Photo: John Scrace

33206 pulls out of Clapham Junction with the 0812 to Kensington Olympia in August 1982.
Photo: John Scrace

33107 and one 4TC unit comprise the 1510 from Salisbury seen approaching Waterloo in August 1983 with the unit leading.
Photo: John Scrace

33033 is pictured at Ponthir with the 1510 service from Cardiff to Crewe during April 1983.
Photo: John Scrace

33114 competes with the town's motoring fraternity for road space as it travels at walking pace toward the Quay Station in Weymouth with the 0940 Boat Train from Waterloo. This view was taken in July 1983.
Photo: John Hypher

33056 'The Burma Star' heads the VSOE 'The Beaulieu Belle' through Horsham with the 1032 Special from Victoria to Brockenhurst on 19th May 1984.
Photo: John Scrace

33049 is pictured at East Croydon with empty Royal Train stock on its way from Tattenham Corner to Wolverton in June 1984.
Photo: John Scrace

One unusual round trip on Saturdays, comprising the first taste of a 33/1 and 4TC in push-pull mode on the service, ran during the summer of 1984. It originated via a Bournemouth area diagram and ran from Weymouth at lunchtime, returning from Westbury mid afternoon. Their last two summer Saturday seasonal appearances in 1988/9 were also push-pull operated via Bournemouth area workings.

The May 1984 timetable revealed another unusual new Crompton working on weekdays from Westbury to Weymouth Quay together with a Sunday trip to the Quay from Bristol Temple Meads. These weekday trains were dated, with the empty coaches coming from Bristol for a 21.10 departure to Weymouth and the Quay. On Sundays the trains started from Bristol at 20.30, running direct to the Quay. With the new October timetable, further trips to the Quay on the same timings ran on Fridays until March, but on Mondays to Thursdays only ran from January until March. The Sunday journeys from Bristol finished at the beginning of January. The fill-in trips to Weston-super-Mare continued until 1987 and included a few through trains to and from Portsmouth Harbour.

Throwing any remaining regional inhibitions to the wind, June 1981 marked the introduction of the 33s to the inter-regional service between the Western and London Midland regions from Cardiff to Crewe. This time it was the turn of the resident class 25s to be sacrificed to make way for their Southern cousins along this 139 mile route. Locomotives for this service were diagrammed via the Portsmouth line on a three day cyclic basis to enable servicing at Eastleigh Depot to be carried out. One interesting fill-in working associated with this service was the use during the small hours of the morning of a nocturnal Crompton between Crewe and Stoke on Trent on a mail train. Becoming even more adventurous, May 1985 saw the 33s on the Cardiff - Crewe service forging onwards to pastures new with a return trip to Bangor along the North Wales coast on Mondays to Saturdays. At the same time a return journey to Manchester Piccadilly was also introduced with the outward leg commencing at Swansea on weekdays and Cardiff on Saturdays but the autumn timetable brought Saturdays into line with the rest of the week. Quite often on Wednesdays, the return journey between Crewe and Bangor was double headed with an ex-works class 37 or 47 on a running-in turn from Crewe Works. The 33 was not on power but ticking over only with the pilot locomotive being separately manned and actually hauling the train. The Manchester service later attracted a Sunday afternoon Crompton working between Cardiff and Manchester, with a simultaneous journey from Manchester to the Principality. But starting with the summer 1986 timetable, the latter was replaced by a class 47 while the former commenced from Swansea.

33042 is pictured arriving at Llandudno Junction in May 1985 with the 1417 from Bangor to Cardiff.

Photo: John Scrace

33025 'Sultan' running incognito minus nameplates and badges along the picturesque Welsh coastline at Ferryside with the 1125 Milford Haven to Swansea in May 1984.
Photo: John Hypher

Even more Crompton surprises were unveiled with the new summer 1986 timetable. The Monday to Saturday return journeys between Crewe, Bangor and Cardiff were extended beyond Bangor to Holyhead on the Isle of Anglesey. Also, the weekday relief trips which had been commonplace the previous summer between Crewe and Llandudno were put on a regular footing for the season with a through Cardiff - Llandudno service, the train returning to Crewe and then later back to Cardiff. The Swansea - Manchester service however was only Crompton hauled on weekdays, the Saturday operation having been handed over to class 47 haulage. But all this was too good to last and at the conclusion of the summer timetable the class 33 activity on the Cardiff - Crewe line, North Wales and the North West ceased.

Turning their attentions towards West Wales, and ousting their English Electric class 37 counterparts in the process, the Cromptons started to run alongside DMUs and class 47s on the scenic and picturesque 72 mile Swansea - Carmarthen - Milford Haven service from May 1982. They also headed boat trains along the 73 mile route to Fishguard Harbour which connected at the terminal there with ferries to Ireland. Some early variants to the norm particularly at weekends comprised trips from Cardiff or Port Talbot to Fishguard Harbour and from Port Talbot to Milford Haven. Journeys between Swansea, Cardiff and Bristol became a regular feature during the class' stay in Wales, a few of these continuing for a while after the Cromptons had ceased running in West Wales. Other duties involved the class on trips between Milford Haven and Cardiff or Bristol Temple Meads as well as spending a spell on a late night Paddington service between Milford Haven and Cardiff. A token number of through trains between Portsmouth Harbour and Swansea were also featured in the timetable. Class 33 activity on the West Wales services came to an end with the introduction of the summer 1986 timetable.

Ever onwards, the class made further inroads into Western Region territory by spearheading their way through Devon - again. This came more as a renewed acquaintance rather than a carving out of yet new territory as the 33s had been a familiar part of the scene during the 1970s and on freight traffic over many years. Their re-emergence started with the October 1982 timetable and saw them running again on a number of journeys between Exeter, Barnstaple, Newton Abbot and Paignton, meaning farewell to the resident class 31s. At just under 40 miles in length, the line from Exeter to Barnstaple is for the most part single line, a token being collected on the outward journey at Crediton and handed back to the signalman on the return trip. Travelling the other way, the route from Exeter St. Davids to Paignton extends for some 27 miles and takes in the popular resorts of Dawlish, Teignmouth and Torquay. The Cromptons with their Mk. 1 stock were a very welcome sight along the famous coast at Dawlish and were just as much at home there as their famous and often photographed steam and diesel-hydraulic predecessors. Locomotives worked in the main to and from the line via the Meldon Quarry trains and also from the

33042 waits at Manchester Piccadilly prior to working the 1345 to Cardiff in February 1986.
Photo:Paul Llewellyn

The driver of 33011 hands back the single line token to the signalman at Crediton. The train was the 1607 Barnstaple to Exeter seen during July 1984.
Photo: John Hypher

33044 is pictured at Folkestone Warren with the 1642 Dover to Bescot in May 1985.
Photo: John Scrace

33206 passes through the gypsum intake at Northfleet Cement Works, unloading the 1130 from Mountfield during May 1986.
Photo: Keith Dungate

33042 and snowplough ADS 70227 were caught by the camera at Clapham Junction out of season in June 1986!
Photo: John Scrace

Brighton or Bristol line as regards weekend Barnstaple workings. Summer Saturdays in particular saw the class working many of the trains on the Barnstaple line which contrasted with the occasional and token journeys performed on Sundays. A variety of other passenger trains arose out of the 'Exeter' diagrams during their term which included trips between Exeter and Plymouth and an evening through train between Paignton and Cardiff which initially ran on Mondays to Thursdays but later operated additionally on Fridays as well. The Paignton leg was relatively short lived and this service subsequently ran from Exeter instead until 1987. An early morning weekday journey from Bristol Temple Meads to Plymouth also ran for while as did a weekday nocturnal working between Bristol and Exeter. Summer 1984 produced a couple of interesting workings out of Plymouth, one of which was a dated Monday to Thursday service to Newton Abbot and Paignton. The other was an afternoon Friday only service which took the Crompton right through to Paddington. This Friday train was also repeated during the summer of 1985. A local working during July and August 1986 saw the class performing an early evening weekday return service between Exeter and Honiton. The only other diagrammed class 33 passenger work that summer was on the Saturday Barnstaple timetable, the conclusion of which officially ended the 33s renewed acquaintance in the area apart from freight and vans movements. However, undiagrammed appearances were made along some of their old haunts in Devon the following summer.

Meanwhile, the Portsmouth line diagrams were producing a variety of associated workings. The early 1980s brought a short-lived early morning weekday return journey for the Cromptons, running between Cardiff and Gloucester which was soon extended to Cheltenham. October 1982 saw the introduction of another short-lived Compton hauled train which ran on weekdays from Swindon to Bristol Temple Meads but this only survived until the following May.

Taunton became an early favourite for the 33s with several journeys being run from Bristol. At least one through working on a Sunday was from Taunton through to Portsmouth Harbour. Although rostered class 33 duties finished in May 1987, they continued to make appearances right to the end.

Headcode 99 denoted the Brighton - Bristol - Cardiff service which initially comprised weekend workings only with one trip in each direction on Saturdays and Sundays. The frequency however was later extended from the summer 1984 timetable to include weekdays as well. These continued to work on a one round trip basis until the Sprinters took over in May 1988.

In addition to those mentioned previously, a number of other short term assignments were allocated to the Cromptons during the 1980s. These included a lunchtime Fridays only journey from Portsmouth Harbour to Leeds which the locomotive ran as far as Birmingham New Street. The Sunday return trip from Yorkshire was also taken over at Birmingham during the early evening with the class being diagrammed on these trains until May 1984. Leeds was again featured on a dated inter-regional morning service from Weymouth during the summer of 1983 and was diagrammed for a 33/1 as far as Reading, returning with the southbound working at lunchtime.

Another Fridays only journey which survived only a matter of months under Crompton command was a lunchtime train from Portsmouth Harbour to Exeter which ran for the duration of the winter 1986/87 timetable.

Following the wholesale withdrawal of the class from much of its passenger work in May 1988, a surprise came in the shape of a Saturdays only morning working from Portsmouth Harbour to Waterloo which survived for a year. This working was a little unusual in that it ran with electric multiple units to the capital.

Eastern Region passengers were treated to class 33 haulage, albeit for one day only, in January 1986 when 33038 operated a round trip between Liverpool Street and Kings Lynn followed by a round trip between Liverpool Street and Cambridge. These were normal service journeys and this locomotive happened to be the only one available to haul these trains complete with a suitably qualified driver.

33051 rushes towards Bournemouth with the 1035 'Bournemouth Belle'. It is pictured at Lymington Junction during July 1987.
Photo: John Scrace

Bradford-on-Avon is a pretty town in Wiltshire and provides some splendid scenic views along the course of the railway in the area. 33026 approaches the town in April 1988 with the 1305 Cardiff to Portsmouth Harbour.
Photo: John Scrace

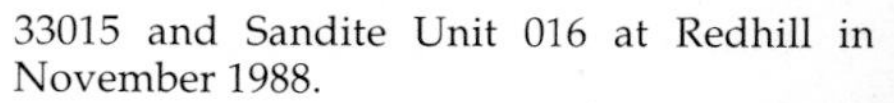

33015 and Sandite Unit 016 at Redhill in November 1988.
Photo: John Scrace

Despite having been ousted from the Exeter line, the 33s remained on the Waterloo-Salisbury-Yeovil 'shorts' in a mix of both push-pull and conventionally hauled formations. Additionally, a handful of through workings survived from Waterloo to Exeter as well as the usual weekend forays between Brighton and Exeter where the stock continued on to further West of England destinations behind alternative motive power. An all-time regular for the Cromptons was the weekdays 16.38 journey from Waterloo which initially ran as far as Yeovil Junction but from May 1983 was extended to Exeter. This normally returned at around 21.00 for Salisbury on Mondays to Thursdays and Basingstoke on Fridays. Another regular was a summer Saturdays through working from Waterloo which left early morning and returned at lunchtime from Exeter. Summer 1983 however produced a push-pull formation on this train with a 33/1 and 8TC working through to Exeter. The 1987 season saw this train start even earlier, but from Salisbury, and return some three hours earlier for London. Sundays also achieved a regular through working in the shape of the 13.45 to Waterloo. These continued until 1987 but the Salisbury and Yeovil 'shorts' continued until May 1989 when the class 50s took over the operation. A 'top and tail' push-pull working commenced in May 1988 with the 08.39 Yeovil to Waterloo. This arrived at Salisbury with the TC unit leading where it was joined to another TC unit with a 33/1 at the front. The onward formation consisted of a 33/1+4TC+4TC+33/1! Throughout the years, the Cromptons often deputised for the class 50s and indeed continued after they had officially been removed from the service. Before leaving this line, further interest was added during the 1980s in the shape of two weekday peak-hour formations from Waterloo which included an electric multiple unit as far as Basingstoke. Whilst others also ran from time to time, these two comprised regular workings running roughly an hour apart during the afternoon rush-hour with the first train going to Salisbury and the latter running to Yeovil Junction. The EMUs which were at the rear of the train were detached at Basingstoke and continued their separate journeys along the Bournemouth line.

The Saturdays only Brighton - Exeter trains continued as usual with the traditional summer double-headers being eagerly sought out by enthusiasts. These were enhanced in May 1983 by a Fridays only working which left late morning from Brighton bound for Exeter and which survived until September 1986. An additional Saturdays only trip was introduced from May 1987 in the shape of a double-headed early morning journey from Exeter to Hove. At the same time however, the return Saturdays journey from Exeter to Brighton was discontinued. After many years on the service, the Cromptons said their final farewell in 1988.

Freight workings for the Cromptons have been many and varied. Some of the more significant trains which were often double-headed were those originating from Merehead and Whatley Quarries in Somerset and Meldon Quarry in Devon on stone traffic together with cement movements from Wiltshire. Others comprised the Willesden to Millbrook Freightliners and Northfleet to Luton cement trains. Making do with a single locomotive were oil workings from Fawley and also

33027 'Earl Mountbatten of Burma' and 33055 pass through Lewisham during September 1987 with the 1000 Purley to Cliffe.
Photo: John Scrace

from Furzebrook in Dorset.

Although now some 30 years old, the 33s are heavily utilised on front line freight duties on the heavy Channel Tunnel construction trains. Indeed, it was this traffic which had a significant bearing in reprieving a proportion of the class beyond their projected withdrawal dates and brought about further classified overhauls at Eastleigh. Commencing in 1988, regular double-headed traffic developed from the TML segment manufacturing complex at the Isle of Grain to the construction site at Shakespeare Cliff and also aggregates movements from Cliffe Brett Marine to the TML distribution terminal at Sevington. Minestone traffic from Snowdown Colliery (Kent) to the distribution terminal at Sevington is also Crompton hauled but normally by a single locomotive. However, on Sundays during June and July 1989 the trips from Grain to Shakespeare Cliff became triple-headed. This was due to engineering work being carried out on the Dartford Loop, Swanley to Otford Junction and the Petts Wood to Orpington lines along their usual route. The diversion which required the extra power entailed a run-round at Hoo Junction followed by a re-route via Sittingbourne and Canterbury East to Dover and Shakespeare Cliff.

Their freight duties have taken the Cromptons to many yards both on the Southern and on other regions too. Among these were Clapham, Crawley, Redhill, Three Bridges, Tonbridge, Grain, Hoo, Northfleet, Cliffe, Southampton, Eastleigh, Woking, Salisbury, Westbury and Exeter. In addition, by the very nature of freight movements, they were regular visitors to the London area yards of adjoining regions. While their appearances these days are somewhat fewer and in decline, they can still be seen in many locations on both freight and departmental duties.

Vans movements were once a familiar activity entrusted over many years to the 33s. Many of these were nocturnal and not only confined to Southern metals, the Western Region being a significant beneficiary during the 1980s. These ran on a network of movements across the region but, alas, almost none of these now remain rostered for the class.

With the grounding of the class 155 Sprinter fleet in December 1988, 33/1s and 4TCs came to the rescue on some of the workings on the Portsmouth - Cardiff service, particularly between Salisbury and Portsmouth Harbour as required during the crisis. Weekend track engineering work also brought the class back into the limelight when they hauled Waterloo - Weymouth 'Wessex Electrics' via the non-electrified diversionary route between Basingstoke and Eastleigh via Romsey and Chandlers Ford during the winter of 1988/9.

The only diagrammed passenger workings for the 33s from October 1989 were the afternoon 'Kenny Belles'. These had been run by class 73 Electro-diesels with 4TC units since the previous May, often with a locomotive at each end of the train. However, with the new timetable the service reverted back to 33/1 operation but this only lasted for a matter of days before going over to Western Region DMUs, thus drawing to a close diagrammed passenger service for the class.

33042 is seen at Woking on test from Eastleigh Works following its CEM at the end of March 1989.

Photo: John Scrace

Detailed below are some examples of Crompton diagrams which illustrate the type of duties which these locomotives performed and the extent of their travels within a day's work. These relate to Summer 1984.

WeekdaysClass 33/0 — Eastleigh Depot

Day 1

0254	Eastleigh Depot Light Engine / ECS	
05.50	Portsmouth Harbour to Bristol Temple Meads	arr 08.52
14.55	Bristol Temple Meads to Weston-super-Mare	arr 15.26
16.20	Weston-super-Mare to Bristol Temple Meads	arr 16.55
17.20	Bristol Temple Meads to Taunton	arr 18.32
19.00	Taunton to Bristol Temple Meads	arr 20.13
21.45	Bristol Malago Vale to Cardiff Canton (ECS)	arr 23.10

Day 2

04.20	Cardiff Canton to Newport (Light engine)	arr 04.40
05.00	Newport to Bristol Temple Meads (Vans)	arr 05.36
09.15	Bristol Temple Meads to Taunton	arr 10.26
11.10	Taunton to Bristol Temple Meads	arr 12.20
17.14	Bristol Temple Meads to Brighton	arr 20.28

Day 3

04.50	Brighton to Worthing	arr 05.10
05.50	Worthing to Brighton Yard (ECS)	arr 06.20
08.30	Brighton to Bristol Temple Meads	arr 11.48
14.40	Bristol Temple Meads to Cardiff	arr 15.27
16.15	Cardiff to Bristol Temple Meads	arr 17.02
18.10	Bristol Temple Meads to Portsmouth Harbour	arr 20.50
21.32	Light engine to Eastleigh Depot.	

Fridays Class 33/0 — Hither Green Depot

04.30	Selhurst Depot to Clapham Yard (Light engine)	arr 05.03
05.18	Clapham Yard to Hove (ECS)	arr 06.50
11.14	Brighton to Exeter St. Davids	arr 15.19
17.00	Exeter to Bristol Bath Road (Light engine)	arr 20.00
22.20	Bristol Temple Meads to Exeter St. Davids	arr 00.01

Saturdays

03.00	Exeter St. Davids to Barnstaple (Vans)	arr 04.32
06.25	Barnstaple to Exeter St. Davids (Vans)	arr 07.35
08.15	Exeter St. Davids to Barnstaple	arr 09.25
10.00	Barnstaple to Exeter St. Davids	arr 11.03
12.45	Exeter St. Davids to Barnstaple	arr 13.43
14.10	Barnstaple to Exeter St. Davids	arr 15.07
15.26	Exeter St. Davids to Barnstaple	arr 16.29
16.45	Barnstaple to Exeter St. Davids	arr 17.41

Sundays

13.45	Exeter St. Davids to Waterloo	arr 17.14
19.28	Waterloo to Clapham Yard (ECS)	arr 19.43
20.10	Clapham Yard to Waterloo (ECS)	arr 20.19
21.12	Waterloo to Clapham Yard (Light engine)	arr 21.20
22.45	Clapham Yard to Victoria (Light engine)	arr 23.00

WeekdaysClass 33/1 Eastleigh Depot

Day 1

03.39	Eastleigh Depot to Salisbury (Light engine)	arr 04.28
05.10	Salisbury to Gillingham (ECS)	arr 05.36
05.45	Gillingham to Basingstoke (Pushing)	arr 07.04
08.34	Basingstoke to Salisbury	arr 09.21
09.35	Salisbury to Waterloo (Pushing)	arr 11.12
12.10	Waterloo to Salisbury	arr 13.52
15.10	Salisbury to Waterloo (Pushing)	arr 16.49
17.00	Waterloo to Salisbury (With EMU to Basingstoke)	arr 18.45
19.50	Salisbury to Westbury (For fuelling)	
21.30	Westbury to Salisbury (Light engine)	arr 22.05
22.23	Salisbury to Basingstoke	arr 23.13

Day 2

06.35	Basingstoke to Salisbury	arr 07.26
07.55	Salisbury to Waterloo (Pushing)	arr 09.34
10.10	Waterloo to Salisbury	arr 11.53
13.10	Salisbury to Waterloo (Pushing)	arr 14.48
14.57	Waterloo to Clapham Yard/Junction (ECS)	
16.00	Clapham Junction to Kensington Olympia (Pushing)	arr 16.08
16.12	Kensington Olympia to Clapham Junction	arr 16.20
16.25	Clapham Junction to Kensington Olympia (Pushing)	arr 16.33
16.37	Kensington Olympia to Clapham Junction	arr 16.45
16.50	Clapham Junction to Kensington Olympia (Pushing)	arr 16.58
17.03	Kensington Olympia to Clapham Junction	arr 17.11
17.15	Clapham Junction to Kensington Olympia (Pushing)	arr 17.23
17.27	Kensington Olympia to Clapham Junction	arr 17.35
17.47	Clapham Junction to Waterloo (ECS)	arr 17.59
18.10	Waterloo to Yeovil Junction (With EMU to Basingstoke)	arr 20.48
21.22	Yeovil Junction to Salisbury	arr 22.14
22.26	Salisbury to Eastleigh Depot (Light engine)	arr 23.15

With just a few minutes between trips, 33103 and 4TC No. 431 prepare to leave Kensington Olympia for the next shuttle back to Clapham Junction in September 1984.
Photo: John Hypher

33205 and 33056 are pictured at Faversham in April 1988 with the 0808 Ridham Dock to Betteshanger Colliery empties.

Photo: Rodney Lissenden

With the run down of the class in prospect initially and then becoming a reality, the demand for Crompton hauled railtours grew during the latter years of the 1980s and took the class far and wide in their travels.

Listed below are a selection of some of the railtours and specials which the Cromptons have headed over the past three or four years.

January 1986	33051 & 33062	The Wirral Withershins to Rock Ferry
November 1986	33202 & 33207	The Eden Serpent to Carlisle
December 1986	33202 & 33209	The Conwy Crompton Pullman to North Wales
February 1987	33025 & 33062	Valley Basher II to South Wales
October 1987	33031 then 33112	Templecombe Ltd to Liskeard
December 1987	33207 & 33059	The Pembroke Coast Pullman to West Wales

In addition, on Network Day in October 1987, 33102 and 4TC 8027 worked on the Watford Junction to St. Albans Abbey branch.

May 1988	33112 & 33026	Crompton Farewell to Carmarthen
May 1988	33103	Push-pull Farewell. Freight lines in Hants/Dorset
September 1988	33209, 33051 & 33112	Coupled Crompton in Kent/Sussex/Hants
October 1988	33211 & 33207	Crompton Cornish Farewell to Penzance
October 1988	33031 & 33033	Crompton Cornish Swansong to Penzance
May 1989	33119 & 33106	The Tortuous Tortoise to Meldon Quarry
June 1989	33058	The Coalville Cobbler to Coalville

Inter-City Diesel Day in May 1989 saw 33021 and 33022 running between St. Pancras and Leicester. Weymouth Centenary Gala Day took place at the end of December 1989 and following a special from Bournemouth to Weymouth, 33117 performed a series of push-pull trips between Weymouth and Weymouth Quay. Unfortunately however, the loco failed before the conclusion of the programme.

Finally, The Anniversary Aggregate made a tour of lines in Kent in January 1990 with Railfreight liveried 33050 and 33051 in charge.

November 1985 was a notable date for the 33s as it witnessed the end of an era with the closure of Hither Green as a TMD. This brought with it the transfer of its entire resident fleet of Cromptons to Stewarts Lane TMD. Thus another chapter in the history of the class came to a close as some of the Cromptons had never been based anywhere else from new.

Just over a year after its naming, 33056 'The Burma Star' sustained serious damage after colliding with an engineers train between Salfords and Earlswood in October 1981. It was out of service for over a year and re-entered traffic in January 1983 following major repairs at Slade Green. Not so lucky was 33104 which was eventually written-off following an accident near Micheldever in January 1985.

This was the first withdrawal for over six years and was followed progressively by others either through accident or fire damage or through the generally poor condition of the locomotive concerned. With classified overhauls having ceased in May 1986 and the projected run-down of the class being actioned, Cromptons fell by the wayside at a steady rate. Whilst there have been a handful of reinstatements to traffic, these have normally been achieved through the sacrifice of parts from fellow donor locomotives. To date only 56 of the original 98 remain in the active fleet. The remainder have either been broken up or are mouldering having been stripped for spares and await their last journey to the cutters torch. One lucky loco to have an assured future is 33034 which has been purchased for preservation. This at present is a non-runner but who knows what the future might hold?

One of four dedicated Dover shunting locos, 33205 is pictured at Dover Admiralty Pier during April 1989.

Photo: Martyn West

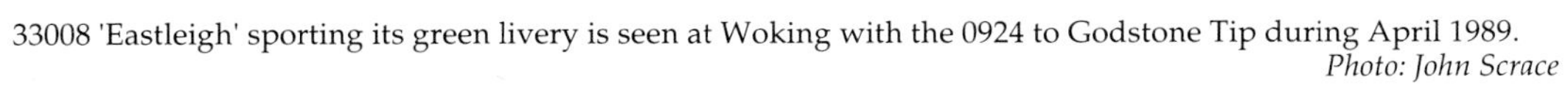
33008 'Eastleigh' sporting its green livery is seen at Woking with the 0924 to Godstone Tip during April 1989.
Photo: John Scrace

Chapter 6 What's in a Name ?

A total of ten Cromptons have been named since 1980, adding not only a splash of colour and further interest to the fleet, but also recognising people and places pertinent to the Southern, its territory and work. Two names have been transferred between locomotives resulting in all three sub-classes having achieved at least one named member.

33008 'Eastleigh'

33008 started the ball rolling for the class when it was named 'Eastleigh' at Eastleigh Station on 11 April 1980. This was in recognition of the railways' long standing association with the town spanning almost 90 years. The Mayor of Eastleigh, Councillor Pat Hallifax was invited to unveil the nameplate at a special ceremony attended by the local MP Sir David Price, leading civic dignitaries and officials and hosted by the Southern Region's General Manager Mr John Palette.

Eastleigh (then called Bishopstoke) can trace its initial railway origins back to 1839 when the London and Southampton Railway opened its section of line between Southampton and Winchester. Half a century later in 1891, the London and South Western Railway opened a carriage works at Eastleigh (now demolished) for the building and repair of carriages and wagons. This was followed in 1910 by the opening of the locomotive works (still extant) which apart from carrying out repairs to engines produced such well known Southern classes as the King Arthur, Lord Nelson, Schools, Merchant Navy, West Country and Battle of Britain.

The skills and expertise of the workforce were diverted to a great extent to the production of armaments during the second world war. These included heavy gun barrels, parts for Spitfires, tanks, torpedoes and assault landing craft.

Following the demise of steam, a programme of rationalisation was instituted which included modernisation and re-equipping at the locomotive works. This rendered the carriage works surplus to the revised requirements and it was closed during 1968, repairs to electric and diesel-electric units being carried out on the locomotive site. Among the products of the carriage works during its latter years were the 'Hastings' and 'Hampshire' diesel-electric multiple units and the six class 73/0 Electro-diesels.

The vast majority of overhauls, conversions and major works attention performed on the Cromptons have been carried out at Eastleigh and it was fitting that one of their 'charges' should carry a tribute to the men, their skills and the town that has produced and repaired both locomotives and rolling stock for several generations.

33008 'Eastleigh' at Waterloo Station just three days after its naming on 14 April 1980.
Photo: John Scrace

Above: 33008 was the first Crompton to be named and this view shows the Mayor, Cllr. Pat Hallifax, unveiling 'Eastleigh's nameplate on 11 April 1980.
Photo: Courtesy Eastleigh & South Hants Weekly News

Left: 33025 'Sultan' and 33202 standing at Crowborough Station during engineers track occupation in July 1984.
Photo: Keith Dungate

Close up of 33025's nameplate and badge.

Photo: John Scrace

33025 'Sultan'
33114 'Sultan'

Thursday 6th August 1981 witnessed the fifth Crompton naming, this time at Portsmouth Harbour Station. At a special ceremony which took place at 3pm, Captain Austin Lockyer MVO ADC RN, the Commanding Officer of Gosport based HMS Sultan unveiled the nameplate and crest of 33025 and formally named the locomotive 'Sultan'. The crests, made of cast iron, were produced in HMS Sultan's foundry by Chief Marine Engineering Artificer Charlie Bathe and painted by Marine Engineering Artificer Terence Maloney, truly magnificent achievements by both men. A third crest was also produced which is on display at the base.

This event marked the Silver Jubilee of HMS Sultan, the Royal Navy's School of Marine Engineering and was attended by some fifty officers and ratings from the establishment together with Mr John Palette, General Manager of the Southern Region and other senior BR officials. 33025 was chosen by number to reflect the 25th anniversary of the establishment. HMS Sultan, the sixth ship or shore based establishment to carry the name since 1775 is responsible for training engineers to the highest calibre. They are trained in the operation, running and maintenance of ships' main propulsion machinery which includes the boilers, steam turbines, diesel engines and all electrical machinery as well as the main electrical supply system and the wide variety of auxiliary equipment found in modern warships. Today's modern, sophisticated, hi-tech equipment requires highly skilled specialist engineers and technicians and HMS Sultan provides such men for the fleet.

At least three previous locomotives have carried the name 'Sultan' which is a Moslem sovereign. The first was a Great Western Railway broad gauge 4-2-2 'Iron Duke' class 8ft single which was built in November 1847 and withdrawn in 1874. This was followed by a GWR 3001 class 2-2-2 single no. 3020 built in April 1892 and converted to 4-2-2 two years later before being withdrawn in 1908. 33025s immediate predecessor was Western Region diesel-hydraulic 'Warship' class locomotive no. D848 which entered service in April 1961 and, following a remarkably short service life of only eight years, was withdrawn in March 1969.

Upon its own withdrawal in February 1988, 33025s nameplates and crests were transferred to class 33/1 no. 33114 without ceremony in April 1988, this being the second and last of the push-pull locomotives to be named. Its glory however was short lived as 33025 was reinstated during November 1988 and shortly afterwards re-united with its rightful identity.

33114 'Sultan' during its brief spell as a 'namer' seen at Eastleigh Works Open Day in September 1988.
Photo: Paul Llewellyn

33027 'Earl Mountbatten of Burma' eases the Royal Train into Ashford Station on its way to the Lydd branch during May 1986.
Photo: Keith Dungate

33027 'Earl Mountbatten of Burma'
33207 'Earl Mountbatten of Burma'
33056 'The Burma Star'

On 5 September 1979 the funeral train bearing the late Lord Mountbatten slowly pulled away from Waterloo station on its journey to Romsey in Hampshire. This was the sad and final journey of one of the outstanding figures of our time, a fearless leader, a man of wisdom and vision and a man of deep compassion. A year later the same two locomotives which had hauled this train were chosen to carry both names and shields in honour of Lord Mountbatten and of The Burma Campaign of the second world war.

Accordingly, 33027 and 33056 were named 'Earl Mountbatten of Burma' and 'The Burma Star' respectively at a special ceremony held at Waterloo Station on 2 September 1980. Countess Mountbatten of Burma was invited to unveil the nameplate and shield of 33027 'Earl Mountbatten of Burma' and Lord Mountbatten's daughter, Lady Pamela Hicks, was similarly invited to name 33056 'The Burma Star'. BR Chairman Sir Peter Parker and Southern Region General Manager Mr. John Palette hosted the ceremony which also included a parade of the Royal British Legion and The Burma Star Association's National Standards.

world war he commanded HMS Kelly until it was sunk during a concentrated attack by Junkers dive bombers. In 1942, Mountbatten was appointed Chief of Combined Operations responsible for planning the invasion of Europe, following which in 1943 he was appointed Supreme Allied Commander, South East Asia with the daunting task of driving the Japanese out of Burma. His outstanding strategies during the Burma Campaign not only brought about their liberation but also the surrender of the Japanese over which he presided. The Burma Star Medal was awarded to all who served in the Burma Campaign between December 1941 and September 1945 and this is depicted on the shield carried by 33056.

In 1947 he became the last Viceroy of India and was responsible for the smooth transfer of power to India and Pakistan. It is a reflection of the high esteem in which he was held by the Indian people that he was chosen to be their first Governor General, an appointment which he held for a year. He was created an Earl and once again returned to the Royal Navy as Commander-in-Chief, Mediterranean, before

Close up of 33027's nameplate and shield.

Photo: John Scrace

A third copy of the 'Earl of Mountbatten of Burma' nameplate was produced and is on display in the Mountbatten Exhibition at Broadlands, Hampshire.

Born in 1900, Louis Mountbatten was a great-grandson of Queen Victoria. He joined the Royal Navy as a midshipman during the first world war and went on to Cambridge at its conclusion. His naval career continued and in 1934 he obtained his first command as captain of the destroyer HMS Daring, later moving on as captain of the Wishart. During the second

becoming First Sea Lord in 1955. His final appointment was that of Chief of the Defence Staff. In retirement Lord Mountbatten travelled extensively but always found time to take an active interest in many charities and their work.

In August 1989 the nameplates and shield from 33027 were removed and transferred to Railfreight liveried class 33/2 No. 33207 without ceremony; this being the only 'Slim Jim' to have been named thus far.

33207 'Earl Mountbatten of Burma' at Clapham Junction during March 1990. This name was previously carried by 33027.

Photo: Paul Llewellyn

33056 'The Burma Star' rests at Norwood Junction in August 1983.

Photo: John Scrace

33050 'Isle of Grain' resplendent in its new Railfreight livery at Clapham Junction in May 1988.

Photo: John Scrace

33050 'Isle of Grain'
33051 'Shakespeare Cliff'

The first dedicated Railfreight Construction sub-sector class 33s to be named were 33050 and 33051 which became 'Isle of Grain' and 'Shakespeare Cliff' respectively. These two locomotives comprise part of the class to be allocated for use in connection with the construction of the Channel Tunnel and this was reflected in the names chosen for them.

Appropriately, the ceremony was staged at the Transmanche-Link (TML) Production Facility at the Isle of Grain and took place at 11.00 on Monday 16 May 1988. Both TML and Railfreight officials were in attendance together with a number of invited guests. Sir Nicholas Hunt, the Deputy Managing Director of Eurotunnel was invited to unveil the nameplate of 33050 followed by Railfreight Director, Mr Colin Driver who performed the honours for 33051. Both Cromptons resplendent in their new Railfreight livery then double-headed a segment train away from the site. The nameplates carried by these locomotives departed from the usual practice of having a red background in being painted light blue instead. Above them are situated small 'TML' logo roundels.

Pre-cast concrete segments for the Channel Tunnel are manufactured at the large TML production complex at the Isle of Grain and transported by rail to the main construction site at Shakespeare Cliff near Dover. These segments are used to line the tunnels and are put into place by the boring machines which in addition to cutting by means of a rotating head also remove the spoil. Over 700,000 concrete and cast iron segments will be used in the construction process.

Shakespeare Cliff situated on the Kent Coast between Dover and Folkestone marks the starting point of the UK tunnelling operations both landwards towards the terminal site near Folkestone and seawards towards Calais. It is anticipated that the 31 mile tunnel will open in 1993 with through passenger and freight services together with specially designed rail shuttles for cars, caravans, coaches and lorries opening up endless trade and travel possibilities between the UK and the rest of Europe.

Three tunnels will cross the Channel. Two of these will carry trains and will be linked by a separate service tunnel placed between them.

Close up of 33050's nameplate and TML roundel.

Photo: Simon Moore

Close up of 33051's nameplate and TML roundel.

Photo: Martyn West

33052 'Ashford'

Within a matter of weeks of the first member of the class being named, the second in the shape of 33052 was swiftly ushered into the spotlight. It was named 'Ashford' at the town's railway station on 15 May 1980 by the Mayor, Councillor H E Apps. As with Eastleigh the town of Ashford in Kent is rich in railway history stretching back well over a century to 1842 with the arrival of the South Eastern Railway. This location was chosen to site a new works for the building and repair of locomotives, carriages and wagons and opened in 1847, with the first locally built steam locomotive being outshopped in 1853. During the second world war Ashford was subjected to enemy air-raids which, apart from causing damage to the works, sadly took its toll in human lives too.

The strange looking Bulleid austerity Q1 class 0-6-0 locomotives were Ashford products which rather interestingly were numbered 33001 - 33040. During the early 1950s the works also produced the Bulleid designed diesel-electric locomotives 10101 - 10103 whereas the previous decade saw the construction of the famous 'booster' electric locomotives 20001 - 20003.

Carriage production ceased in 1928, this function being transferred to Lancing, but the building and repair of wagons continued until 1983 with the works finally closing in June 1984. Steam locomotive production had ceased during the late 1940s and repairs in 1962, this work being transferred to Eastleigh. Under the BREL banner until its closure, Ashford Works built and exported wagons to a number of countries around the world.

33112 'Templecombe'

Following a period of some six years where no further class 33 namings had taken place, 33112 broke the spell to be christened 'Templecombe'. It also created two landmarks in the process as this was the first push-pull class 33/1 to be named and the only Crompton to carry two shields. Having been postponed from Saturday 17 October 1987 owing to the widespread hurricane damage and consequent disruption only days previously, 33112 was duly named at Templecombe Station two weeks later on the 31st. The nameplate and two shields, one depicting the London and South Western Railway coat of arms and the other the coat of arms of the Somerset and Dorset Joint Railway, were unveiled by Ian Matthews, Chairman of the Templecombe Station Promotion Group. Gerald Daniels, the well known Salisbury area manager, hosted the event. Following the ceremony 33112 hauled the TSPG charter train to Liskeard, returning to Waterloo at dusk.

The only previous locomotive to carry the name 'Templecombe' was Bulleid West Country class Pacific no. 34098. This was built at Brighton in December 1949 and lost its streamlined casing upon rebuild at Eastleigh in February 1961. Finally withdrawn in July 1967 at the conclusion of steam on the Southern, it was subsequently broken up by a South Wales scrap dealer.

The Templecombe Station Working Committee, formed on 19 March 1982 was successful in its aim to re-open the station which had closed on 6 March 1966. After an extensive campaign, the station was re-opened on October 3 1983 and since then the group (subsequently re-named the Templecombe Station Promotion Group) has remained in existence to promote the facilities from the station. A close working relationship exists between the Southern Region and the TSPG and as a result following a request from the group, the General Manager of the SR, Mr Gordon Pettitt agreed to 33112 being named 'Templecombe' in view of the success of the station due in no small way to the TSPG's efforts" to quote his reply.

This particular locomotive was chosen for a number of reasons. Firstly, in immaculate ex-works condition following an intermediate overhaul at Eastleigh, it had hauled the 'Somerset and Dorset Rambler' railtour in May 1987 which had been promoted by the TSPG. This locomotive, by now a firm favourite, was also frequently used on the Waterloo - Yeovil service and its number 112 was coincidentally the number on the mileage post at Templecombe, being 112 miles from Waterloo. 33112s glory was however short lived as it was withdrawn a year later as a result of collision damage sustained at Salisbury.

33112 'Templecombe' at Southampton during April 1988 showing its two shields to advantage.
Photo: John Scrace

Chronological table of namings

Number	Name	Named	De-named	Renamed
33008	Eastleigh	11-4-80	-	-
33052	Ashford	15-5-80	-	-
33027	Earl Mountbatten of Burma	2-9-80	Aug.1989	To 33207
33056	The Burma Star	2-9-80	-	-
33025	Sultan	6-8-81	Feb.1988	Dec.1988
33112	Templecombe	31-10-87	Nov.1988	-
33114	Sultan (ex 33025)	4-88	Dec.1988	To 33025
33050	Isle of Grain	16-5-88	*	*
33051	Shakespeare Cliff	16-5-88	-	-
33207	Earl Mountbatten of Burma	8-89	-	Ex 33027

* Nameplates and roundels removed while locomotive was stored and repaired at Stratford during 1988/9.

During 1983/4, 33025 ran for a while without crests and also totally anonymously bereft of both nameplates and crests. These were subsequently restored.

Ceremony to name the locomotives 'Earl Mountbatten of Burma' and 'The Burma Star'.

Courtesy British Rail (Southern)

Ceremony to name the Locomotives
"Earl Mountbatten of Burma"
and
"The Burma Star"

ON TUESDAY 2 SEPTEMBER 1980
AT WATERLOO STATION.

Programme

11 15
Coffee with Mr. John Palette, General Manager, in Officers' Mess
(entrance opposite Platform 21)

11 50
Assemble on Platform 11 for naming ceremony

11 55
Parade of the Royal British Legion and The Burma Star
Association's National Standards

12 00
Mr. Palette will introduce Sir Peter Parker MVO,
British Railways Board Chairman
Sir Peter will invite the
Countess Mountbatten of Burma
to name Locomotive No. 33027
"Earl Mountbatten of Burma"
and Lady Pamela Hicks
to name Locomotive No. 33056
"The Burma Star."

12 15
Short informal period for inspection of locomotives and
press/television shots

12 30
Guests leave by special coach for luncheon at the Charing Cross
Hotel (Canterbury Room) Tel: 01-839 7282

14 30
Cars – Charing Cross Hotel

Limited Souvenir Programme for the naming of locomotive 33112 'Templecombe'. Due to severe hurricanes that swept the country, 33112 was not in fact named until a fortnight later on 31 October 1987.

Courtesy: Templecombe Station Promotion Group

LIMITED
SOUVENIR PROGRAMME

FOR THE
NAMING
OF

LOCOMOTIVE

33112
"Templecombe"

AT
TEMPLECOMBE STATION
17th OCTOBER 1987

No. 037

Chapter 7 A Splash of Colour

During their lifetime, the Cromptons have been quite colourful machines ranging from their original rich green livery, through several years of rail blue to the current Railfreight and Departmental liveries based on various shades of grey. In between, several variations and adornments were introduced on a number of locomotives at various stages which helped keep interest in the fleet alive. Needless to say, while a few of these were official, many were unofficial and as such tended to last for only a relatively short while.

Each of the type 3s was delivered in a dark green livery with light grey roofs and cream window surrounds together with cream bands amidships and red buffer beams. The British Railways lion and wheel motif was carried on each side and the locomotive numbers were positioned under each of the cabside windows, giving four in total.

In common with other diesel classes, small yellow warning panels began to appear around 1962/3 and were painted on the front ends beneath the cream bands, although many were still running without these long afterwards. Some of the green Cromptons in fact went a stage further and, prior to sporting the new blue livery, were painted with the now familiar all yellow fronts with yellow cab window surrounds from the late 1960s. The cream bands on the cab doors and under the cab windows on these particular locomotives initially remained intact but these soon disappeared leaving the band running along the bodysides only between each pair of doors.

1966 heralded a totally new corporate image for the railways which meant that green was out and blue was in. Accordingly, the first type 3 to emerge in its new blue coat was D6521, a freshly converted push-pull loco which was outshopped from Eastleigh Works in November 1966. All-yellow front ends and cab windows surrounds were featured as standard, apart from which the rest of the locomotive was

This view of D6551 illustrates the small yellow warning panel applied to the green livery. This loco together with an all-blue 4TC unit is seen at Hamworthy Junction with the 1745 Bournemouth to Weymouth in August 1969.
Photo: John Scrace

D6566 with an empty Royal Train is pictured at Tattenham Corner in May 1968 and shows the loco with the all-yellow front and shortened white bands.
Photo: John Scrace

D6522 photographed at Purley in May 1968 shows it in the new blue livery.
Photo: John Scrace

blue with the buffer beams painted black. The new white BR 'arrow' symbols were sited in place of the numbers under each of the cabsides while the D65xx numbers, white in colour and more rounded, were relocated to the bodysides adjacent to the cab doors or radiator grilles. In order to accommodate these new BR 'arrows', the BRCW makers plates were moved to a lower position on the cabsides. Following the cessation of steam in 1967, 'D' prefixes were gradually dropped leaving just the 65xx numbers. The ongoing programme of repainting the Cromptons into blue livery continued apace and was completed in 1971.

Next on the agenda was the TOPS renumbering scheme which took place from late 1973 until the spring of 1974. Under the renumbering, each Crompton received a new number prefixed by 33 and instead of carrying four numbers (2 per bodyside) this was reduced to two, one per side at diagonally opposite ends of the main bodysides.

No further changes occurred until 1980 when a revised colour scheme was adopted for named locomotives. 33027 and 33056 were the first recipients to be adorned in their new coats in September 1980 which were standard blue and yellow but with light grey roofs and red buffer beams. Their nameplates, as with their previously named counterparts, had silver letters on a red background. 33025 followed suit with the new colours when it was named the following year. The two previously named Cromptons 33008 and 33052 ran however in standard colours, 33008 eventually being brought into line with the others, but 33052 retaining its standard blue throughout.

33012 made something of a surprise appearance in what can only be described as a 'Lone Ranger' livery. It made its debut during December 1981 complete with grey roof, black cab window surrounds, wrap-round yellow cabs and red buffer beams. Its bodysides remained in standard blue but carried one BR 'arrow' symbol along each bodyside rather than one on each cabside. While its numbers remained in-situ, it carried additional small black numbers centrally located on the front ends of the locomotive. It survived in this unofficial guise until August 1982 when it was repainted back into standard colours following classified overhaul.

Other unofficial paint jobs were applied to a small number of the push-pull Cromptons in the shape of white cab window surrounds. 33101 was the first to appear during the summer of 1982 and was followed by 33105/107 and 119. This splash of white certainly enhanced the locomotives appearance and suited them well. However, the yellow paintbrush had other ideas and all were put back into standard livery in due course, the last to be done being 33105 which managed to survive until the end of 1984.

'Templecombe' (33112) broke the 'namer' livery mould in October 1987 by having a one-off livery to celebrate its naming. It appeared in standard blue but with the addition of black front cab windows surrounds at each end and black cab roofs. It is surprising what a difference this made to 'Templecombe's' appearance and indeed ensured instant recognition. This was the only class 33 to carry two shields under each nameplate and the plates retained silver letters on a red background.

Sectorisation of the railways brought with it not only separate businesses and accountability but also a new public image for most of the sectors and a new range of colour schemes for both locomotives and rolling stock within the owning sectors. Two of the new liveries, those for the Railfreight and Departmental fleets, have been applied to the Cromptons. The first to be so treated were three 'Slim Jims' (33203/205 and 206) used on Dover Docks shunting duties which were painted in Railfreight Speedlink colours during March 1988. Thus far these are the only 33s to have received this particular version of the new Railfreight livery. These were swiftly followed in May 1988 by a pair of standard 33s (33050 and 33051) painted into Railfreight Construction livery and which were also named during the same month. Since these were outshopped, further examples of both the standard and 'Slim Jim' varieties have been similarly treated following CEM overhauls at Eastleigh Works.

Railfreight livery consists of two shades of grey on the bodysides. These comprise a medium grey from the cantrail to the base of the engine room windows and a light grey to the base of the body. Cab doors, cab window surrounds and the main radiator grilles and buffer beams are black, while the roof is painted in a very dark grey. The front ends below cab window level are painted yellow and the scheme is finished off by a thin orange band which goes round the locomotives at guttering and cantrail level. The last three digits of the locomotive's number are carried on each front end in small back numerals and are placed off-centre to the right under the top right hand lamp bracket. Black locomotive numbers are carried only under the driver's cab windows on each side. These were fairly small on the first Cromptons to be treated but on later repaints larger numerals were used.

Speedlink examples carry large yellow and red decals on each side, more or less midway between the engine room access door and the driver's cab door. Additionally, a thin red and yellow strip is located behind the second man's cab door which extends from the top of the light grey paint to the base of the body.

Construction locomotives on the other hand carry large blue and yellow decals in the same position as the Speedlink machines and likewise carry a blue and yellow strip to the rear of the second man's door. Unlike the Speedlink locomotives however, those in Construction colours have a large polished metal 'arrow' symbol positioned under the driver's cabsides. Named Cromptons in the Construction colours have silver lettering picked out on a blue background instead of the traditional red. Large metal Oast House depot symbols were fitted to two Construction machines, 33050 and 33207 during

With the disappearance of steam, 'D' prefixes were discontinued. This view of 6558 at Redhill in April 1973 shows this alteration.

Photo: John Scrace

33012 in its 'Lone Ranger' livery is seen at Horsham in April 1982.

Photo: John Scrace

SULZER

SOUTHERN REGION

One of the B.R.C. & W. built Type 3 locomotives is shown working a goods train on the Hastings line near Battle, Sussex. Power is provided by a Sulzer 8LDA28 diesel engine which develops 1,550 b.h.p. at 750 r.p.m.

This Sulzer advertisement dating from the early 1960s shows one of the 'Slim Jims' in original green livery working a freight train.

Courtesy: Sulzer Diesel

33005 wearing standard blue livery awaits its next tour of duty at Bristol, Bath Road TMD in June 1983.
Photo: John Hypher

33056 'The Burma Star' is pictured in ex-works condition following accident repairs. This attractive livery applied to named Cromptons suited them very well.
Photo: John Hypher

Outshopped in this striking livery from Stewarts Lane in October 1988, 33023 passes Edenbridge with the 1430 Tonbridge to Preston Mails during November 1988. By the end of the month, the yellow paintbrush had removed the white window surrounds.
Photo: Keith Dungate

Sporting its new Civil Engineers Departmental grey livery, 33065 waits to leave Redhill Yard with a Departmental train bound for Three Bridges in April 1990.
Photo: Keith Dungate

The new Departmental livery now incorporates wide yellow bands along the bodysides. 33103 is seen in this modified scheme at Tonbridge in August 1990.
Photo: Keith Dungate

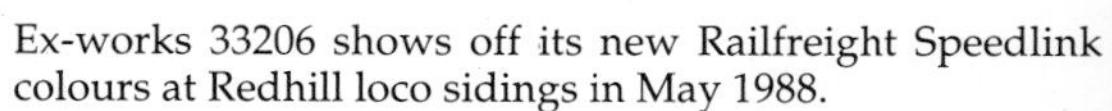

Ex-works 33206 shows off its new Railfreight Speedlink colours at Redhill loco sidings in May 1988.
Photo: Keith Dungate

33050 'Isle of Grain' is pictured in Railfreight Construction colours in August 1989. Note the Oast House depot symbol under the second man's cabside window.

Photo: David Robinson

33008 is pictured in the second of its four green livery versions at Bournemouth during July 1986. It was preparing to leave for Waterloo with the 1545 'Bournemouth Belle'.

Photo: John Hypher

83301 (formerly 33115) sporting its Mainline colours in February 1990.

Photo: Class 33 Locomotive Club Collection, Courtesy: British Rail

Showing its Departmental strip and full set of mini-snowploughs, 33004 stands at Three Bridges in February 1989. Note also the 73A plate on the front.
Photo: John Scrace

33112 'Templecombe' was given black front window surrounds when named. It is seen at Southampton during April 1988 on a trip from Three Bridges to Redbridge.
Photo: John Scrace

the summer of 1989. Located on the second man's cabsides, the symbols are diamond shaped and depict silver oast houses against a black background.

Turning now to the Civil Engineer's Departmental Sector, the base colour for the fleet is a medium grey. As with the Railfreight locomotives, cab doors, cab window surrounds and buffer beams are painted black. Roofs are painted the same grey as the bodysides. The front ends below cab window level are yellow and as usual a thin orange band extending around the locomotive at guttering and cantrail level is also featured. Again, as with the Railfreight machines, small black numbers are located in the same position on the front ends. White locomotive numbers are positioned under the driver's cab windows while the large polished metal rail 'arrows' are sited under the second man's cabside windows. However, 33103 at least carries its metal 'arrows' under its numbers on the driver's cabsides. No decals or other markings are carried on 33s belonging to this sector. However, as this book was going to press, 33103 was given a yellow band along its bodysides from cantrail level to a position just below the engine room windows and others in the fleet have followed suit.

The Channel Tunnel Project can be thanked for the emergence of a Crompton in Mainline colours. 83301, formerly 33115 was released from RFS Industries of Doncaster in February 1990 following modifications and the fitting of TGV bogies of the type to be used by the power cars which will run between London, Paris and Brussels. Being unpowered, 83301 will be coupled behind a class 73 electro-diesel for the duration of the tests, some of which it is anticipated will take place in service on the Gatwick Expresses.

The mainline livery is similar in many respects to that of Inter-city locomotives but apart from its locomotive numbers, 83301 carries no other decals, emblems, lettering or British Rail 'arrows'. It consists of a dark grey roof and dark grey bodysides which extend the full length of the locomotive. This continues down the body to a point just below half way where it meets a thin white stripe followed by a slightly wider red band, both of which also extend the full length of the locomotive. Underneath this to the base of the body is a light grey band upon which the locomotive numbers are sited in small black numerals near the bottom of the driver's cabsides. All yellow front ends with white lamp brackets are featured together with a thin orange stripe which goes round the locomotive along the guttering and cantrail. The radiator grilles have been plated over and carry the relevant colours across these plates.

33008 'Eastleigh' must qualify as the most liveried Crompton. It started life like all the others in green livery and as with its compatriots went into the new blue colour scheme. It then eventually received the revised colours for named 33s before being outshopped in a special green livery following its classified overhaul at Eastleigh Works in May 1986. This machine was the last standard locomotive to receive an Intermediate overhaul. This special green livery was applied in exactly the same format as that for named locomotives i.e. light grey roof, yellow front ends and cab window surrounds but with the rest of the body in green. Buffer beams however were painted black and the now standard orange stripe along the guttering and cantrail was applied. Numbers and BR 'arrows' were placed in their usual positions. It wasn't long though before this underwent a gradual metamorphosis into what was to closely resemble its 1960s green format. This took place in three stages during 1986, the first of which was to paint the buffer beams red and apply a thin white band amidships which ran the whole length of the body each side of its 'Eastleigh' nameplates. This was followed shortly afterwards by the addition of white cab window surrounds. The next and final stage saw the removal of the BR 'arrows' and the placing of its locomotive numbers under the driver's cabside windows. The yellow between the cab windows and the roof was painted green and the white band extended round the front ends as well. To facilitate this, green was applied to each end of the locomotive round its now reduced rectangular yellow warning panel. British Railways lion and wheel motifs were placed along each bodyside (one per side) below the white band towards no. 1 and no. 2 ends respectively. The metamorphosis complete, the finished result bore fairly close similarities to its original livery. However, following unclassified repairs at Eastleigh during March 1990, 33008 emerged in Departmental grey, thus ending almost four years of a unique and welcome flashback to the way things used to be. Upon repaint, it retained the red background to its nameplates.

33023 is worthy of special mention as its depot repaint at Selhurst in 1988 created something of an anomaly. Although un-named it was given a similar blue livery to the named locomotives complete with red buffer beams and grey roof but with the addition of white cab window surrounds and blue strips above the cabside windows. Within a month however, the white had disappeared together with the blue

33205 was renumbered 33302 for a short while during 1988. It was photographed at Ashford in August 1988 in this guise.
Photo: John Scrace

1985 saw a few of the class decorated with cats. One such example was 33058 whose paintwork seems a little the worse for wear.
Photo: Paul Llewellyn

New Forest ponies made their short-lived debut during 1987. An equestrian 33033 is seen during the summer.

Photo: Paul Llewellyn

strips and the window surrounds reverted back to standard yellow. The red buffer beams and grey roof remained intact and the locomotive is still running in these colours.

The now standard orange stripe which follows the guttering over the cab windows and then along the bodysides at cantrail level started to appear on the class during the summer of 1986 and has progressively been applied to most of the remaining fleet. Locomotive class data transfers made their debut during early 1969 followed by depot allocation transfers around 1974. Red coloured high voltage warning flashes on a white background were applied in pairs on the front ends of the Cromptons from mid 1981 and the mini-snowploughs which hitherto had been painted black were outshopped in yellow from the latter part of 1982. Departmental flashes in yellow with yellow diagonal lines and incorporating the letters SR (for Southern Region) were introduced during the summer of 1988 and appeared under the second man's cabside windows on a few of the 33s. 33061 was the last Crompton to carry BRCW makers plates on its cabsides and during the latter years of its life the background to these was standard blue with red lettering. Following overhaul during the summer of 1984 however, these plates were blue but the lettering was picked out in white shortly afterwards. This locomotive, together with 33119, also carried oval 'Rebuilt Slade Green 1982' plates following collision repairs at Slade Green Depot. These were located on the cabsides.

A variety of unofficial adornments, additions and replacements were also added to a number of the Cromptons during recent years. The first rash of these began to appear during 1985 in the shape of white cats, red buffer beams and small hand painted front end black numbers. The cats usually sat beside the locomotive data transfers but only a small number of locomotives received this attention with the cats and black numbers generally being left to wear away. Unofficial black numbers have since appeared sporadically on a few other members of the class. 1987 was also a good year for decorations, this time with New Forest ponies appearing on the upper bodysides of a handful of Cromptons, particularly the push-pull variety. These were swiftly removed and none lasted for more than a matter of weeks. 33056 was also given star treatment when it ran for a while with thin parallel white bands along its bodysides. These were placed above and below its nameplates and extended along the bodysides finishing just before the cab doors. Again, these didn't last long and were soon removed. The same year, 33117 was treated to OM (Old Oak Common) allocation transfers in place of its official EH ones and 33109 received yellow WD (Wimbledon) allocation transfers as applied to electric multiple units. Oval 73A plates also started to be fitted to the front ends of Stewarts Lane allocated locomotives. These had silver characters picked out on a red background but latterly those machines in Railfreight colours have received a blue background to their plates. Some of the push-pull Cromptons received their old numbers in white along their bodysides during the last months of the class on the Bournemouth - Weymouth service, the survival rate of these too being fairly short. During 1989 33039 carried a painted 73C on one of its ends. Oval in shape, it had white characters on a black background. 33108 also received the unofficial name 'Corina' on one of its sides. It was a stick-on name with silver letters on a red background. This was short lived and was soon removed. One other unofficial numbering which took place during 1987 was the placing of small white '6580' numbers under the second man's cabside windows of 33119 together with black '6580' numbers placed centrally on the front ends.

During the course of their lives, a number of Cromptons ran in service with experimental components and modifications. These were denoted on small plates which were fixed to the driver's cab doors for the duration of the experiment. A few examples of those which occurred during the 1980s are shown below.

33105	Exp.No. DL 689	Engine fitted with Napier SAO turbocharger
33049	Exp.No. DL 414	Evaluation of silicon rubber hose on cooling water system
33049	Exp.No. DL 566	Evaluation of exhaust manifold with bellows joints
33050	Exp.No. DL 505	Plastic coating of erosion plugs in fuel pumps
33050	Exp.No. DL 480	Upper main reservoir units of glass reinforced plastic.

Appendix 1 Table of Locomotive Details

ORIGINAL NO.	TOPS NO.	BRCW NO.	INTO SERVICE	ALLOCATIONS (i)	MINI PLOUGHS (ii)	LAST OVERHAUL	SECTOR 9/90 (iii)	LIVERY 9/90 (iv)	WITHDRAWN	DISPOSAL	NOTES
D6500	33001	DEL 92	1/60	73C 1/60, 70D 1/66, EH 5/73	Yes	11/83			3/88	Cut up Eastleigh 2/89	Accident Liss 3/88
D6501	33002	DEL 93	2/60	73C 2/60, 70D 10/65, EH 5/73	No	3/90	DCSM	G			
D6502	-	DEL 94	3/60	73C 3/60	No				5/64	Cut up Itchingfield 7/64	Accident Itchingfield 3/64
D6503	33003	DEL 95	3/60	73C 3/60, 70D 10/65, EH 5/73	Yes	5/84			8/87	Cut up Eastleigh 9/90	Accident Dormans 7/87
D6504	33004	DEL 96	3/60	73C 3/60, 34G 2/61, 73C 2/61, 71A 9/62, 70D 9/63, 73C 4/64, 70D 11/64, EH 5/73, SL 10/88	Yes	7/85	FASB	B			
D6505	33005	DEL 97	4/60	73C 4/60, 71A 9/62, 70D 9/63, EH 5/73	No	6/83			6/87	Vic Berry Leicester 9/90	Fire damage 6/87
D6506	33006	DEL 98	4/60	73C 4/60, 71A 9/62, 70D 9/63, EH5/73, SL 2/89	No	2/85	FASB	B			
D6507	33007	DEL 99	5/60	73C 5/60, 70D 10/65, EH 5/73	No	12/82			12/86	Cut up 4/87 Eastleigh	Accident Chatham 12/86
D6508	33008	DEL 100	5/60	73C 5/60, 71A 9/62, 70D 9/63, 73C 4/64, 70D 4/65, EH 5/73	Yes	5/86	DCSM	G			Named Eastleigh 4/80
D6509	33009	DEL 101	5/60	73C 5/60, 70D 10/65, EH 5/73, SL 3/89, EH 9/90	No	3/85	DCSA	B			
D6510	33010	DEL 102	6/60	73C 6/60, 70D 2/66, EH 5/73	No	9/83			4/88	Cut up 3/89 Eastleigh	
D6511	33101	DEL 103	6/60	73C 6/60, 70D 1/66, EH 5/73	No	8/87	DMSA	B			Push-pull 6/67
D6512	33011	DEL 104	6/60	73C 6/60, 71A 7/63, 70D 9/63 EH 5/73, SL 10/88	No	5/83			3/89		
D6513	33102	DEL 105	6/60	73C 6/60, 70D 5/67, EH 5/73	No	7/87	DCSM	B			Push-pull 10/67
D6514	33103	DEL 106	7/60	73C 7/60, 70D 4/66, EH 5/73	No	12/87	DCSM	G			Push-pull 10/67
D6515	33012	DEL 107	7/60	73C 7/60, 70D 10/65, EH 5/73, SL 2/89	No	4/86	FASB	B			Withdrawn 9/87 Reinstated 1/88
D6516	33104	DEL 108	7/60	73C 7/60, 70D 4/66, EH 5/73	No	9/83			12/85	Cut up Slade Green 12/85	Push-pull 5/67 Accident Mitcheldever 1/85
D6517	33105	DEL 109	7/60	73C 7/60, 34E 12/61, 73C 12/61, 70D 2/66, EH 5/73	No	4/86			10/87	Vic Berry Leicester 9/90	Push-pull 4/67 Accident 10/87
D6518	33013	DEL 110	8/60	73C 8/60, 70D 4/66, EH 5/73, SL 2/89	Yes	10/84			3/89		Fire damage

ORIGINAL NO.	TOPS NO.	BRCW NO.	INTO SERVICE	ALLOCATIONS (i)	MINI PLOUGHS (ii)	LAST OVERHAUL	SECTOR 9/90 (iii)	LIVERY 9/90 (iv)	WITHDRAWN	DISPOSAL	NOTES
D6519	33106	DEL 111	8/60	73C 8/60, 70D 4/66, EH 5/73, SL 9/90	No	1/87	DCSA	B			Push-pull 3/67
D6520	33107	DEL 112	9/60	73C 9/60, 71A 7/63, 70D 9/63, EH 5/73	No	11/86			5/89		Push-pull 2/67 Accident Holton Heath 4/89
D6521	33108	DEL 113	9/60	73C 9/60, 71A 7/63, 70D 9/63, EH 5/73	No	10/85	DCSA	G			Push-pull 11/66
D6522	33014	DEL 114	9/60	73C 9/60, 70D 2/66, 73C 3/68, 70D 9/68, EH 5/73	No	12/84			2/86	Cut up 9/86 Eastleigh	Accident Theale 1/86
D6523	33015	DEL 115	9/60	73C 9/60, 71A 7/63, 70D 9/63, EH 5/73	Yes	8/84			7/89		Fire damage 7/89
D6524	33016	DEL 116	10/60	73C 10/60, 71A 7/63, 70D 9/63, EH 5/73, SL 12/87	No	11/85			10/89		Fire damage 8/89
D6525	33109	DEL 117	10/60	73C 10/60, 71A 7/63, 70D 9/63, EH 5/73	No	6/85	DMSA	B			Push-pull 10/67
D6526	33017	DEL 118	10/60	73C 10/60, 71A 7/63, 70D 9/63, EH 5/73	No	2/84			1/88		Accident Wishford 1/88
D6527	33110	DEL 119	10/60	73C 10/60, 71A 7/63, 70D 9/63, EH 5/73	No	9/86	DCSM	B			Push-pull 4/67
D6528	33111	DEL 120	10/60	73C 10/60, 70D 12/64, EH 5/73	No	3/84	DCWA	B			Push-pull 11/67
D6529	33112	DEL 121	11/60	73C 11/60, 70D 1/66, 73C 1/66, 70D 3/67, EH 5/73	No	4/87			11/88		Push-pull 7/67 Named 'Templecombe' 10/87 Accident Salisbury 10/88
D6530	33018	DEL 122	11/60	73C 11/60, 71A 9/62, 70D 9/63, EH 5/73	No	5/84			2/88	M.O.D. Moreton -in-Marsh on loan	TDB 968030 9/89
D6531	33113	DEL 123	11/60	73C 11/60, 70D 7/66, EH 5/73	No	11/85	DCWA	B			Push-pull 9/67
D6532	33114	DEL 124	11/60	73C 11/60, 70D 12/64, EH 5/73	No	2/88	DCSM	B			Push-pull 6/67 Named 'Sultan' 4/88 to 12/88
D6533	33115	DEL 125	12/60	73C 12/60, 71A 9/62, 70D 9/63, EH 5/73, SL 10/87, EH 12/87, SL 2/90	No	3/85		M	5/89		Push-pull 8/67 Renumbered 83301 See Note A
D6534	33019	DEL 126	12/60	73C 12/60, 71A 7/63, 70D 9/63, EH 5/73, SL 10/88, EH 9/90	No	1/84	DCSA	B			
D6535	33116	DEL 127	12/60	73C 12/60, 70D 12/64, EH 5/73, SL 10/87, EH 12/87	No	6/85	DMSA	B			Push-pull 3/67
D6536	33117	DEL 128	12/60	73C 12/60, 71A 9/62, 70D 9/63, EH 5/73, SL 10/87, EH 12/87	No	10/86	DCWA	B			Push-pull 5/67

ORIGINAL NO.	TOPS NO.	BRCW NO.	INTO SERVICE	ALLOCATIONS (i)	MINI PLOUGHS (ii)	LAST OVERHAUL	SECTOR 9/90 (iii)	LIVERY 9/90 (iv)	WITHDRAWN	DISPOSAL	NOTES
D6537	33020	DEL 129	12/60	73C 12/60, 71A 7/63, 70D 9/63, EH5/73, SL 2/89	No	5/85	FASB	B			
D6538	33118	DEL 130	1/61	73C 1/61, 70D 7/66, EH 5/73, SL 10/87, EH 12/87	No	6/86	DCSM	G			Push-pull 6/67
D6539	33021	DEL 131	1/61	73C 1/61, 70D 7/66, 73C 3/67, 70D 10/67, EH 5/73, SL 10/88	No	11/88	FASB	RC			
D6540	33022	DEL 132	1/61	73C 1/61, 70D 7/64, EH 5/73, SL 12/87	Yes	2/86			12/89		Accident Headcorn 11/89
D6541	33023	DEL 133	1/61	73C 1/61, 34E 10/62, 73C 11/62, 70D 7/64, 73C 4/65, 70D 10/65, EH 5/73, SL 2/89	No	11/84	FASB	BN			
D6542	33024	DEL 134	2/61	73C 2/61, 70D 7/66, EH 5/73	No	4/83			2/86	Cut up 5/86 Eastleigh	Accident Cardiff 12/85
D6543	33025	DEL 135	2/61	73C 2/61, 70D 9/66, EH 5/73, SL 11/88, EH 9/90	No	1/89	DCSA	BN			Named Sultan 8/81 Withdrawn 2/88 Reinstated 11/88
D6544	33026	DEL 136	2/61	73C 2/61, 70D 12/64, EH 5/73	No	7/89	DCSM	G			
D6545	33027	DEL 137	3/61	73C 3/61, 70D 12/64, EH 5/73, SL 12/87, EH 9/90	Yes	9/85	DCSA	BN			Named Earl Mountbatten of Burma 9/80 De-Named 8/89
D6546	33028	DEL 138	3/61	73C 3/61, 71A 9/62, 70D 9/63, EH 5/73	No	7/84			10/88	Cut up 9/89 Eastleigh	
D6547	33029	DEL 139	3/61	73C 3/61, 70D 9/68, EH 5/73, SL 10/88	Yes	5/84	FASB	B			
D6548	33030	DEL 140	4/61	73C 4/61, 70D 12/64, EH 5/73, SL 2/89, EH 9/90	Yes	4/85	DCSA	B			
D6549	33031	DEL 141	4/61	73C 4/61, 71A 9/62, 70D 9/63, 73C 5/71, 70D 10/71, EH 5/73, HG 9/73, EH 9/74, SL 10/88	No	9/83			2/89		Fire damage 2/89
D6550	33032	DEL 142	4/61	73C 4/61, 70D 10/65, 73C 5/71, 70D 10/71, EH 5/73, HG 9/73 EH 4/75	Yes	11/84			3/87	Cut up 7/87 Eastleigh	Accident Frome 3/87
D6551	33033	DEL 143	4/61	73C 4/61, 70D 12/66, 73C 5/71, 70D 10/71, EH 5/73, HG 7/73, EH 4/75, HG 10/76, EH 11/76, HG 10/77, EH 4/79	Yes	10/88	FASB	RC			

ORIGINAL NO.	TOPS NO.	BRCW NO.	INTO SERVICE	ALLOCATIONS (i)	MINI PLOUGHS (ii)	LAST OVERHAUL	SECTOR 9/90 (iii)	LIVERY 9/90 (iv)	WITHDRAWN	DISPOSAL	NOTES
D6552	33034	DEL 144	4/61	73C 4/61, 70D 10/66, 73C 5/68, 70D 1/69, 73C 5/71, 70D 10/71, EH 5/73, HG 5/73, EH 6/83, SL 12/87	No	1/86			1/88	Privately Preserved 1990	
D6553	33035	DEL 145	5/61	73C 5/61, 34E 7/63, 73C 9/63, 16C 1/64, 73C 1/64, 82C 2/64, 73C 4/64, 70D 1/67, 73C 12/70, 70D 10/71, EH 5/73, HG 5/73, EH 6/83, SL 3/88, EH 5/90	No	11/83	DCSA	B			Withdrawn 10/89 Reinstated 1/90
D6554	33036	DEL 146	5/61	73C 5/61, 70D 1/67, 73C 11/70, 70D 1/72, 73C 4/72, HG 5/73		4/77			7/79	Cut up 10/79 Slade Green	Accident Mottingham 10/77
D6555	33037	DEL 147	5/61	73C 5/61, 70D 1/69, 73C 11/70, HG 5/73, EH 6/83	No	1/85			9/87		
D6556	33038	DEL 148	6/61	73C 6/61, 34E 11/61, 73C 12/61, 71A 9/62, 70D 9/63, 73C 10/65, HG 5/73, EH 6/83 SL 3/88	No	11/82			10/88		Previously withdrawn 9/87 & reinstated 2/88 Accident Snowdown 8/88
D6557	33039	DEL 149	6/61	73C 6/61, HG 5/73, EH 6/83, SL 3/88	No	8/82			5/89		
D6558	33040	DEL 150	6/61	73C 6/61, HG 5/73, SL 11/85, EH 1/86, SL 12/87	No	1/86	FASB	B			
D6559	33041	DEL 151	6/61	73C 6/61, 34G 11/61, 34E 12/61, 73C 12/61, HG 5/73		10/73			11/75	Cut up 6/76 Selhurst	Accident Bricklayers Arms Junction 9/75
D6560	33042	DEL 152	7/61	73C 7/61, HG 5/73, SL 11/85, EH 1/86, SL 3/88	No	2/89	FASB	RC			
D6561	33043	DEL 153	7/61	73C 7/61, HG 5/73, SL 11/85, EH 1/86	No	8/85			9/87		
D6562	33044	DEL 154	7/61	73C 7/61, HG 5/73, SL 11/85	Yes	10/84			9/87	Vic Berry Leicester 9/90	
D6563	33045	DEL 155	7/61	73C 7/61, HG 5/73, SL 11/85	No	4/83			10/87	Vic Berry Leicester 9/90	
D6564	33046	DEL 156	7/61	73C 7/61, HG 5/73, SL 11/85	Yes	3/85	FASB	B			
D6565	33047	DEL 169	8/61	73C 8/61, 70D 10/66, 73C 10/66, HG 5/73, SL 11/85, EH 9/90	No		DCSA				See Note B
D6566	33048	DEL 170	8/61	73C 8/61, HG 5/73, SL 11/85	No	4/85	FASB	B			

33046 awaits departure from Swansea with the 1254 to Fishguard Harbour during November 1985.

Photo: S. Blackman

ORIGINAL NO.	TOPS NO.	BRCW NO.	INTO SERVICE	ALLOCATIONS (i)	MINI PLOUGHS (ii)	LAST OVERHAUL	SECTOR 9/90 (iii)	LIVERY 9/90 (iv)	WITHDRAWN	DISPOSAL	NOTES
D6567	33049	DEL 171	9/61	73C 9/61, HG 5/73, SL 11/85,	Yes	9/84			3/88	Cut up 3/89 Eastleigh	Accident Fratton
D6568	33050	DEL 172	9/61	73C 9/61, 34E 7/63, 73C 9/63, HG 5/73, SL 11/85	No	7/85	FASB	RC			Named 'Isle of Grain' 5/88
D6569	33051	DEL 173	9/61	73C 9/61, HG 5/73, SL 11/85	Yes	10/85	FASB	RC			Named 'Shakespeare Cliff' 5/88
D6570	33052	DEL 174	9/61	73C 9/61, HG 5/73, SL 11/85	No	1/84	FASB	B			Named 'Ashford' 5/80
D6571	33053	DEL 175	10/61	73C 10/61, HG 5/73, SL 11/85	No	10/88	FASB	RC			
D6572	33054	DEL 176	10/61	73C 10/61, HG 5/73, SL 11/85	Yes	6/82			2/86	Cut up 8/87 Eastleigh	Accident Chandlers Ford 12/85
D6573	33055	DEL 177	11/61	73C 11/61, 70D 1/66, 73C 5/67, HG 5/73, SL 11/85	No	9/85			12/89		Accident Headcorn 11/89
D6574	33056	DEL 178	10/61	73C 10/61, HG 5/73, SL 11/85	Yes	12/88	FASB	RC			Named 'The Burma Star' 9/80
D6575	33057	DEL 179	11/61	73C 11/61, HG 5/73, SL 11/85, EH 5/90	Yes	5/90	DCSM	G			Previously withdrawn and reinstated twice 89/90
D6576	-	DEL 180	11/61	73C 11/61					11/68	Cut up 3/69 Eastleigh	Accident Reading
D6577	33058	DEL 181	11/61	73C 11/61, 70D 10/66, 73C 12/66, HG 5/73, SL 11/85	Yes	4/84	FASB	B			
D6578	33059	DEL 182	11/61	73C 11/61, 71A 7/63, 70D 9/63, 73C 9/68, HG 5/73, SL 11/85	Yes	2/82			9/88		
D6579	33060	DEL 183	12/61	73C 12/61, 70D 3/68, 73C 9/68, HG 5/73, SL 11/85	Yes	3/86		B			Under decision following fire damage 3/90
D6580	33119	DEL 184	12/61	73C 12/61, 70D 10/65, 73C 11/65, 70D 10/67, EH 5/73, SL 10/87, EH 12/87	No	4/85			10/89		Prototype push-pull 6/65 Fire damage 7/89
D6581	33061	DEL 185	12/61	73C 12/61, HG 5/73, SL 11/85	No	8/84			6/87	Cut up 11/87 Eastleigh	
D6582	33062	DEL 186	12/61	73C 12/61, HG 5/73, SL 11/85	No	6/84			9/87	Vic Berry Leicester 9/90	
D6583	33063	DEL 187	1/62	73C 1/62, 71A 9/62, 70D 9/63, 73C 10/67, HG 5/73, SL 11/85	No	2/89	FASB	RC			

ORIGINAL NO.	TOPS NO.	BRCW NO.	INTO SERVICE	ALLOCATIONS (i)	MINI PLOUGHS (ii)	LAST OVERHAUL	SECTOR 9/90 (iii)	LIVERY 9/90 (iv)	WITHDRAWN	DISPOSAL	NOTES
D6584	33064	DEL 188	1/62	73C 1/62, HG 5/73, SL 11/85, EH 10/88, SL 11/88	No	12/88	FASB	RC			
D6585	33065	DEL 189	1/62	73C 1/62, 71A 9/62, 70D 9/63, 73C 10/67, HG 5/73, SL 11/85, EH 10/88	No	1/90	DCSM	G			
D6586	33201	DEL 157	2/62	73C 2/62, 73D 7/63, 73C 10/67, HG 5/73, SL 11/85	Yes	6/89	DCSM	G			Slow speed control fitted 9/71
D6587	33202	DEL 158	2/62	73C 2/62, 73D 7/63, 73C 10/67, HG 5/73, SL 11/85	Yes	2/89	FASB	RC			Slow speed control fitted 11/70 Previously withdrawn 2/88 to 11/88
D6588	33203	DEL 159	2/62	73C 2/62, 73D 7/63, 73C 10/67, HG 5/73, SL 11/85	No	12/85	FDIB	RD			Slow speed control fitted 3/72
D6589	33204	DEL 160	2/62	73C 2/62, 73D 7/63, 73C 10/67, HG 5/73, SL 11/85	No	2/89	FASB	RC			Slow speed control fitted 2/71
D6590	33205	DEL 161	2/62	73C 2/62, 73D 7/63, 73C 10/67, HG 5/73, SL 11/85	No	3/86	FDIB	RD			Slow speed control fitted 10/70 Previously withdrawn 9/87 to 12/87 Renumbered 33302 8/88 to 10/88
D6591	33206	DEL 162	3/62	73C 3/62, 73D 7/63, 73C 10/67, HG 5/73, SL 11/85	Yes	11/85	FDIB	RD			Slow speed control fitted 10/71
D6592	33207	DEL 163	3/62	73C 3/62, 73D 7/63, 73C 10/67, HG 5/73, SL 11/85	No	3/89	FASB	RC			Slow speed control fitted 9/69 Named 'Earl Mountbatten of Burma' 8/89
D6593	33208	DEL 164	3/62	73C 3/62, 73D 7/63, 73C 10/67, HG 5/73, SL 11/85	No	9/90	DCSA	G			Slow speed control fitted 9/69
D6594	33209	DEL 165	3/62	73C 3/62, 73D 7/63, 73C 10/67, HG 5/73, SL 11/85	No	6/83			12/88	Cut up 10/89 Eastleigh	Slow speed control fitted 2/70
D6595	33210	DEL 166	4/62	73C 4/62, 73D 7/63, 73C 10/67, HG 5/73, SL 11/85	No	2/85			8/87	Vic Berry Leicester 9/90	Slow speed control fitted 11/69
D6596	33211	DEL 167	4/62	73C 4/62, 73D 7/63, 73C 10/67, HG 5/73, SL 11/85	No	11/84	FDIB	B			Slow speed control fitted 5/70
D6597	33212	DEL 168	5/62	73C 5/62, 73D 7/63, 73C 10/67, HG 5/73, SL 11/85	Yes	9/82			9/87		Slow speed control fitted 7/71

Key

i) Allocations

34E - New England
70D - Eastleigh (code change)
82C - Swindon
34G - Finsbury Park
71A - Eastleigh
EH - Eastleigh
73C - Hither Green
HG - Hither Green
73D - St. Leonards
SL - Stewarts Lane

ii) Mini-ploughs This shows the position during the eighties when changes were rare

iii) Sectors

DCSA - Regional Civil Engineer Southern Pool
DCSM - Regional Civil Engineer Meldon Quarry Pool
DCWA - Regional Civil Engineer Westbury Shunting Class 33 Pool

DMSA - DM & EE Southern Region

FASB - Aggregates Southern Region
FDIB - Dover Link Span

iv) Liveries

B - Blue
RD - Railfreight Distribution
BN - Blue 'namer'
G - Departmental Grey
M - Main Line
RC - Railfreight Construction

Note A For details see 'A Splash of Colour'

Note B 33047 at Eastleigh Works for CEM, expected to be released Oct/Nov 1990 in Departmental Grey livery

Appendix 2 Publicity Material

Cromptons have sometimes been featured on publicity material and the following selection shows examples produced by British Rail and by a local authority.

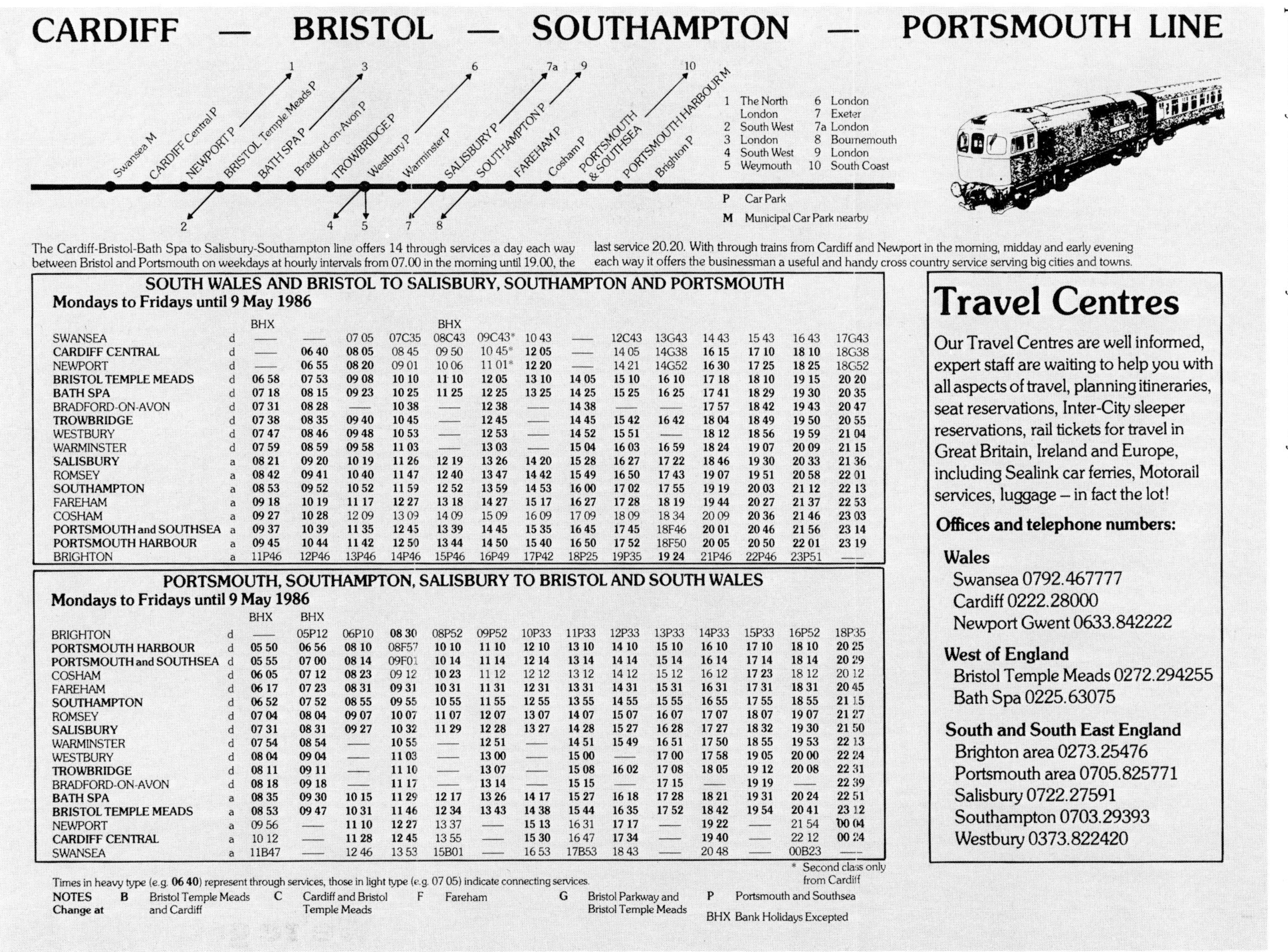

CARDIFF — BRISTOL — SOUTHAMPTON — PORTSMOUTH LINE

Swansea M, CARDIFF Central P, NEWPORT P, BRISTOL Temple Meads P, BATH SPA P, Bradford-on-Avon P, TROWBRIDGE P, Westbury P, Warminster P, SALISBURY P, SOUTHAMPTON P, FAREHAM P, Cosham P, PORTSMOUTH & SOUTHSEA, PORTSMOUTH HARBOUR M, Brighton P

1 The North London
2 South West
3 London
4 South West
5 Weymouth
6 London
7 Exeter
7a London
8 Bournemouth
9 London
10 South Coast

P Car Park
M Municipal Car Park nearby

The Cardiff-Bristol-Bath Spa to Salisbury-Southampton line offers 14 through services a day each way between Bristol and Portsmouth on weekdays at hourly intervals from 07.00 in the morning until 19.00, the last service 20.20. With through trains from Cardiff and Newport in the morning, midday and early evening each way it offers the businessman a useful and handy cross country service serving big cities and towns.

SOUTH WALES AND BRISTOL TO SALISBURY, SOUTHAMPTON AND PORTSMOUTH

Mondays to Fridays until 9 May 1986

		BHX				BHX									
SWANSEA	d	—	—	07 05	07C35	08C43	09C43*	10 43	—	12C43	13G43	14 43	15 43	16 43	17G43
CARDIFF CENTRAL	d	—	06 40	08 05	08 45	09 50	10 45*	12 05	—	14 05	14G38	16 15	17 10	18 10	18G38
NEWPORT	d	—	06 55	08 20	09 01	10 06	11 01*	12 20	—	14 21	14G52	16 30	17 25	18 25	18G52
BRISTOL TEMPLE MEADS	d	06 58	07 53	09 08	10 10	11 10	12 05	13 10	14 05	15 10	16 10	17 18	18 10	19 15	20 20
BATH SPA	d	07 18	08 15	09 23	10 25	11 25	12 25	13 25	14 25	15 25	16 25	17 41	18 29	19 30	20 35
BRADFORD-ON-AVON	d	07 31	08 28	—	10 38	—	12 38	—	14 38	—	—	17 57	18 42	19 43	20 47
TROWBRIDGE	d	07 38	08 35	09 40	10 45	—	12 45	—	14 45	15 42	16 42	18 04	18 49	19 50	20 55
WESTBURY	d	07 47	08 46	09 48	10 53	—	12 53	—	14 52	15 51	—	18 12	18 56	19 59	21 04
WARMINSTER	d	07 59	08 59	09 58	11 03	—	13 03	—	15 04	16 03	16 59	18 24	19 07	20 09	21 15
SALISBURY	a	08 21	09 20	10 19	11 26	12 19	13 26	14 20	15 28	16 27	17 22	18 46	19 30	20 33	21 36
ROMSEY	a	08 42	09 41	10 40	11 47	12 40	13 47	14 42	15 49	16 50	17 43	19 07	19 51	20 58	22 01
SOUTHAMPTON	a	08 53	09 52	10 52	11 59	12 52	13 59	14 53	16 00	17 02	17 55	19 19	20 03	21 12	22 13
FAREHAM	a	09 18	10 19	11 17	12 27	13 18	14 27	15 17	16 27	17 28	18 19	19 44	20 27	21 37	22 53
COSHAM	a	09 27	10 28	12 09	13 09	14 09	15 09	16 09	17 09	18 09	18 34	20 09	20 36	21 46	23 03
PORTSMOUTH and SOUTHSEA	a	09 37	10 39	11 35	12 45	13 39	14 45	15 35	16 45	17 45	18F46	20 01	20 46	21 56	23 14
PORTSMOUTH HARBOUR	a	09 45	10 44	11 42	12 50	13 44	14 50	15 40	16 50	17 52	18F50	20 05	20 50	22 01	23 19
BRIGHTON	a	11P46	12P46	13P46	14P46	15P46	16P49	17P42	18P25	19P35	19 24	21P46	22P46	23P51	—

PORTSMOUTH, SOUTHAMPTON, SALISBURY TO BRISTOL AND SOUTH WALES

Mondays to Fridays until 9 May 1986

		BHX	BHX												
BRIGHTON	d	—	05P12	06P10	08 30	08P52	09P52	10P33	11P33	12P33	13P33	14P33	15P33	16P52	18P35
PORTSMOUTH HARBOUR	d	05 50	06 56	08 10	08F57	10 10	11 10	12 10	13 10	14 10	15 10	16 10	17 10	18 10	20 25
PORTSMOUTH and SOUTHSEA	d	05 55	07 00	08 14	09F01	10 14	11 14	12 14	13 14	14 14	15 14	16 14	17 14	18 14	20 29
COSHAM	d	06 05	07 12	08 23	09 12	10 23	11 12	12 12	13 12	14 12	15 12	16 12	17 23	18 12	20 12
FAREHAM	d	06 17	07 23	08 31	09 31	10 31	11 31	12 31	13 31	14 31	15 31	16 31	17 31	18 31	20 45
SOUTHAMPTON	d	06 52	07 52	08 55	09 55	10 55	11 55	12 55	13 55	14 55	15 55	16 55	17 55	18 55	21 15
ROMSEY	d	07 04	08 04	09 07	10 07	11 07	12 07	13 07	14 07	15 07	16 07	17 07	18 07	19 07	21 27
SALISBURY	d	07 31	08 31	09 27	10 32	11 29	12 28	13 27	14 28	15 27	16 28	17 27	18 32	19 30	21 50
WARMINSTER	d	07 54	08 54	—	10 55	—	12 51	—	14 51	15 49	16 51	17 50	18 55	19 53	22 13
WESTBURY	d	08 04	09 04	—	11 03	—	13 00	—	15 00	—	17 00	17 58	19 05	20 00	22 24
TROWBRIDGE	d	08 11	09 11	—	11 10	—	13 07	—	15 08	16 02	17 08	18 05	19 12	20 08	22 31
BRADFORD-ON-AVON	d	08 18	09 18	—	11 17	—	13 14	—	15 15	—	17 15	—	19 19	—	22 39
BATH SPA	a	08 35	09 30	10 15	11 29	12 17	13 26	14 17	15 27	16 18	17 28	18 21	19 31	20 24	22 51
BRISTOL TEMPLE MEADS	a	08 53	09 47	10 31	11 46	12 34	13 43	14 38	15 44	16 35	17 52	18 42	19 54	20 41	23 12
NEWPORT	a	09 56	—	11 10	12 27	13 37	—	15 13	16 31	17 17	—	19 22	—	21 54	00 04
CARDIFF CENTRAL	a	10 12	—	11 28	12 45	13 55	—	15 30	16 47	17 34	—	19 40	—	22 12	00 24
SWANSEA	a	11B47	—	12 46	13 53	15B01	—	16 53	17B53	18 43	—	20 48	—	00B23	—

* Second class only from Cardiff

Times in heavy type (e.g. **06 40**) represent through services, those in light type (e.g. 07 05) indicate connecting services.

NOTES Change at B Bristol Temple Meads and Cardiff; C Cardiff and Bristol Temple Meads; F Fareham; G Bristol Parkway and Bristol Temple Meads; P Portsmouth and Southsea

BHX Bank Holidays Excepted

Travel Centres

Our Travel Centres are well informed, expert staff are waiting to help you with all aspects of travel, planning itineraries, seat reservations, Inter-City sleeper reservations, rail tickets for travel in Great Britain, Ireland and Europe, including Sealink car ferries, Motorail services, luggage – in fact the lot!

Offices and telephone numbers:

Wales
Swansea 0792.467777
Cardiff 0222.28000
Newport Gwent 0633.842222

West of England
Bristol Temple Meads 0272.294255
Bath Spa 0225.63075

South and South East England
Brighton area 0273.25476
Portsmouth area 0705.825771
Salisbury 0722.27591
Southampton 0703.29393
Westbury 0373.822420

The Western Region produced this timetable for the Severn-Solent Line which featured a drawing of a Crompton, the regular motive power for the service. This drawing is a representation of 33027 'Earl Mountbatten of Burma'.

Courtesy: British Rail (Western)

A Crompton was featured on the front cover of this leaflet produced in connection with the centenary of the Edenbridge - Eridge Line in 1988.

Courtesy: Network South East

A special leaflet was issued by The County of Avon following improvements both to the station and rail service at Keynsham. A named Crompton takes pride of place in heralding the changes which were officially introduced from 30 September 1985.

Courtesy: County of Avon

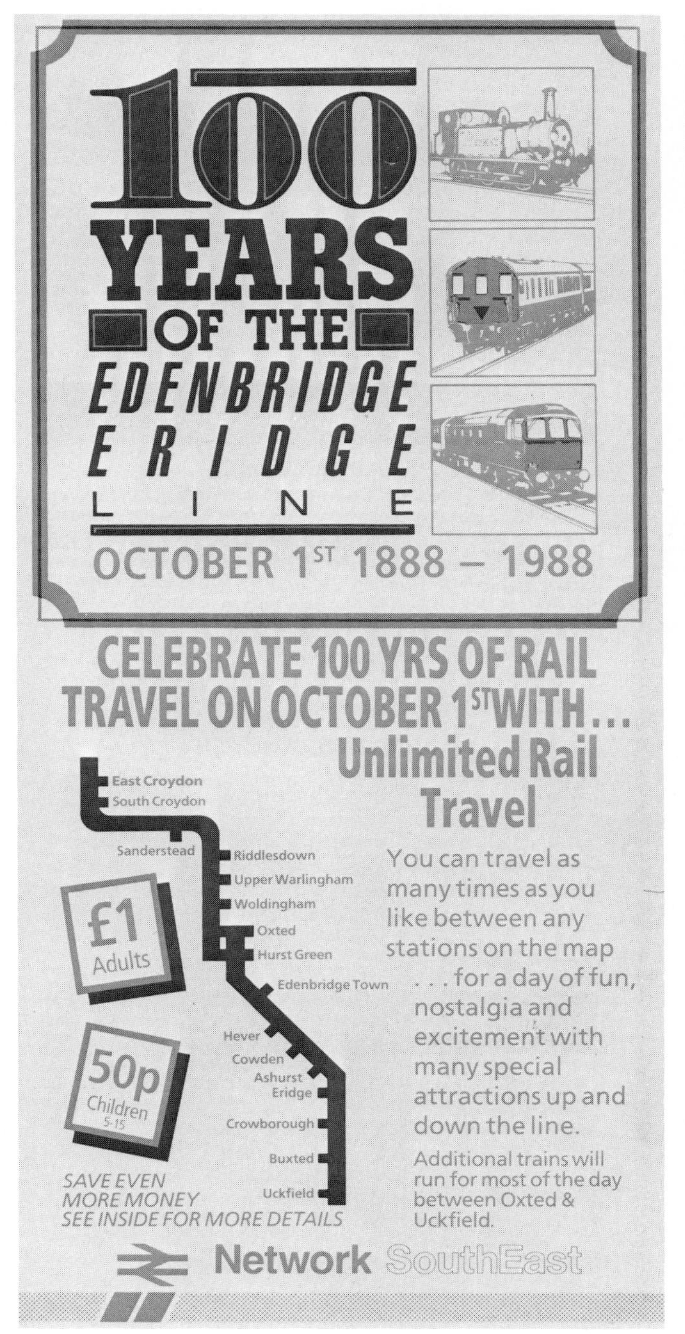

Appendix 3 Class 33 Interest & Preservation Groups

If you have enjoyed this book and would like to keep up to date with the ever changing world of the Cromptons, The Class 33 Locomotive Club will keep you posted. The club is run by enthusiasts for enthusiasts with the aim of providing its members with up to date information on all aspects of the class. The quarterly 'Review' includes:-

* colour photo page
* overhauls
* freight workings
* modifications
* articles
* re-allocations
* livery changes
* withdrawals
* unusual workings
* re-numbering
* namings
* disposals

Club events include works and depot visits as well as social activities, details of which appear in the 'Review'.

For details of membership please write enclosing s.a.e. to:-

Mr P Llewellyn, 48 Alexandra Road, Uckfield, East Sussex TN22 5BE.

Several groups have also been formed with the aim of preserving and running Cromptons in working order on some of the country's preserved railway lines.

These are:-
1) The BRC&W Type 3 Preservation Group
2) The 33/1 Preservation Group
3) The 33/2 Preservation Group

For those who would like further information or would like to become involved in saving some of these fine locomotives for posterity, these groups regularly advertise in the leading railway journals from where their addresses can be obtained. Alternatively, the Class 33 Locomotive Club would be happy to provide this information.

In addition to these, there are other private groups who have similar aims and are seeking to save members of the class also.

Class 33 Models

A number of class 33 locomotive models have been produced by both Lima and Graham Farish representing the standard and push-pull variants together with a range of liveries which these machines have carried over their thirty year span. These have been produced in three gauges and while some of the '00' models have been discontinued it may still be possible to obtain some of these from dealers or from model railway exhibitions.

Lima '0' gauge

Model No.	Loco. No.	Livery	Notes
Not known	Not known	Green	-
Not known	Not known	Blue	-

Lima '00' gauge

Model No.	Loco. No.	Livery	Notes
Not known	Not known	Green	Original Livery
Not known	33024	Blue	-
Not known	33027	Blue 'named'	Earl Mountbatten of Burma
5115	33025	Blue	Fictitious livery for this class and locomotive
5174	33056	Blue 'named'	The Burma Star
5126	33008	Special green	Intermediate livery
5221	33008	Special green	Final variant
5116	33105	Blue	Push-pull
5070	33205	Railfreight Speedlink	Standard loco body but with 'Slim Jim' number
5228	33050	Railfreight Construction	Isle of Grain

Graham Farish 'N' gauge

Model No.	Loco No.	Livery	Notes
8314	D6572	Green	-
8315	33012	Blue	-

Appendix 4 Ever Onwards - The Final Decade?

We have now entered a new decade, possibly the last for the 33s with the remaining fleet under either Railfreight or Departmental ownership. With the introduction of the new Railfreight class 60s to the Southern, particularly on Channel Tunnel trains and the use of other locomotive classes on freight, a gradual run-down of Crompton activity and consequential withdrawals can be anticipated in this sector.

The Departmental Sector on the other hand have in the 33s an ideal locomotive for their purposes. They have sponsored CEMs for the class and, based on current information, it is thought that some of the Cromptons belonging to this fleet may survive to the year 2000. Indeed there are reports, as yet unconfirmed, that ten of this sectors' class 33s will receive names in the near future - watch this space !

Keith Dungate's photograph below shows an optimistic Crompton complete with its GB plates ready for the Channel Tunnel crossing, but I doubt somehow whether it will ever make the trip into Europe ! That would be hoping too much!